HANDBOOK
OF
LAW STUDY

by

FERDINAND F. STONE

Professor of Law and
Director, Institute of Comparative Law
in Tulane University

LITTLE, BROWN AND COMPANY
Boston   Toronto

DEDICATION

To all who ask questions and to all those who seek to help men and themselves to find answers, this book is dedicated. Particularly among these latter are my parents and my law tutor at Oxford, Dr. G. C. Cheshire.

PREFACE

When I was a student in college, and puzzled about whether to go to law school, a friendly and well-meaning adviser recommended that I should read Holmes' *The Common Law.* I did, conscientiously, from beginning to end—and have no recollection that that reading contributed anything to the solution of my problem or much, if anything, to my education. Since studying law, I have read *The Common Law* with more comprehension, I think, and more intellectual profit, I hope. But I remain of the view that it is not the book to be recommended to most persons at the threshold of legal study.

Then what book can be suggested? Of course there are many fine biographies of lawyers and judges, and of statesmen with legal training. And there are novels and trials and other books which will help to depict some of the flavor of legal work. There are books on legal method or law practice which are primarily suitable for the law student who has made most of the decisions which will lead him to become a lawyer. But law teachers, though rather prolific in the production of materials for law school use, have almost completely ignored the problems of the student at the door. Yet such a student can only be advised effectively by a person with legal training. Only a person who has been through the path himself can accurately advise the newcomer what he may expect.

Professor Stone's book meets this need with great wisdom and skill. It is relatively short and thus will not seek to demand too much from the readers for whom it is intended.

We who have spent years in the legal field can easily over-
look how large a number of ideas there are to be absorbed
by the beginner.   The book is well and interestingly written.
There is not a difficult or abstruse passage in it.   But it is
not oversimplified.   The reader is not talked down to.   What
Professor Stone has provided is direct, straightforward exposi-
tion, readily understandable, but all very pertinent and en-
lightening.   The prospective law student will find here much
that will help him to decide, and to prepare for legal study,
and the entering law student will find much that will aid him
on his way as he begins his law school work.   He will not
be overwhelmed, as he might well be, by some of the classics
of legal literature.   He will be better prepared to read the
classics with the background and foundation which are so
skillfully given in this book.

   I am particularly glad that Professor Stone has included
a chapter on the ethical problems confronting the lawyer.
There is naturally and legitimately widespread interest in the
ethical questions of legal practice, among lawyers and laymen
alike.   This is a peculiarly difficult matter to present to the
person who has little legal background.   Professor Stone is
not dogmatic in his presentation.   Yet he points out the basic
problems.   By and large, it may be said, I think, that the
ethics of law practice should not be a matter of rules.   A
lawyer can stick within all the fixed rules and still be a rather
poor representative of his profession.   It is more a question
of a person's standards, and these standards may well require
conduct which is materially above that specified by the few
formulated canons.   Here, as in many other facets of a
lawyer's work, it is not the least that he can get away with
that counts, but the best that he can do that is really important.   The challenge to produce the best that is in them
has brought forth many remarkably fine performances from

lawyers, both in behalf of their clients and in the great field of public service.

In one of Holmes' more colorful passages, he spoke: "When I think thus of the law, I see a princess mightier than she who once wrought at Bayeux, eternally weaving into her dim web figures of the ever-lengthening past,—figures too dim to be noticed by the idle, too symbolic to be interpreted except by her pupils, but to the discerning eye disclosing every painful step and every world shaking contest by which mankind has worked and fought its way from savage isolation to organic social life."   The real lawyer spends a fascinating lifetime in the pursuit and understanding of these figures, occasionally contributing a few to the web through his own thought and effort, and taking legitimately a measure of satisfaction from his personal participation in the great process.   Professor Stone has provided a well planned and soundly written guide for those who are entering into this ancient and honorable field of human endeavor.

ERWIN N. GRISWOLD
Dean and Langdell Professor of Law
Harvard Law School

TABLE OF CONTENTS

1

BY WAY OF INTRODUCTION

There are three kinds of people who need this book and for whom it has been written: the man who is debating whether to study law; the man who is preparing for law study; and the man who has entered law school and stands bewildered on the threshold. Let me hasten to add that it is written for women as well. The early chapters are designed primarily for persons who are weighing the question of law study and for those who, having made a decision, wish to know how to prepare. The later chapters are for those who are already beginning their bout with the law.

This is not a law book in the traditional sense. Rather it is a book by way of introduction to law and lawyers, courts and legislatures. There are two schools of thought about books or courses by way of introduction to law. Some maintain that it is better to throw the victim into deep water to sink or swim. Others maintain that if the beginner is told something of what to expect and of what is expected of him, he will be better able to keep his head above water. Obviously this book follows the latter reasoning. Some floundering about is necessary and to be expected when one is a beginner. There will be good and bad days in law school as in anything else. But through the kind of introduction this book provides many of the unnecessary flounderings and failures can be avoided.

Some books are easy to write because either no one feels

strongly about the subject or the matter is well agreed upon. This has been a difficult book to write because it treats of matters upon which law teachers, old and young practitioners, and judges feel strongly and are by no means in agreement. The law is a majestic theme to be introduced. Whatever one says about it is likely to appear to some as less than enough and to others as a bit too florid. All toastmasters are aware of this dilemma. In this book, we have taken pains to say nothing which is patently false and a good deal which is as close to the truth as we can come.

In such a small book, it is necessary to select only those themes which appear most baffling to the beginner, as viewed from the experience of a teacher. Perhaps no two law teachers would agree upon an exact enumeration of the problems which vex the student. Each speaks from his own experience. The problems which are treated in this book are essential ones which touch the hard core of law study. They have been chosen in the light of the experience of the classroom and of counselling students over many years.

And so, here is the introduction to the law. May it serve to help you to see and, in seeing, to understand. Like all introductions, it is the first step in what may become for you a lasting and rewarding relationship.

"DOCTOR, LAWYER, MERCHANT, CHIEF"

Is Law the Profession for You?

Choosing a profession is a little like choosing a wife. The choice is intended to be a permanent one, and to a marked degree it depends upon the character of the chooser.

In some cases, it is possible to give a vocation a trial before deciding whether it is the one you want and for which you are best suited. But it is not usual to have a "trial go" at the profession of law, because it requires a long period of study and training before you are permitted to try your wings.

The question then is: How can you go about deciding whether law is the profession for you? Certainly it is a question which is capable of being answered, because for centuries men have been making decisions to go into the profession and so far as we know the great majority of them have found it rewarding and satisfying. No test or machine has yet been devised which will decide for you whether you ought to study law. Certain vocational guidance and legal aptitude tests are available which, within reasonable limits, may indicate the direction of your skills. These can be helpful in pointing a direction, but they carry no guarantees. It is a decision which you must make for yourself, and in making it you must act on the best advice obtainable.

The counsel of older members at the bar is helpful. They can tell you of the work which the lawyer does, of the difficulties to be encountered, and of the satisfactions and rewards to be found in the practice. Some of them may tell you that law is an overcrowded profession, usually softening the remark by quoting the old saw that "there is always room at the top." It is likewise useful to talk to law teachers, who can tell you something of the subject matter of law study and of the hazards and pleasures of that study. Some of them may warn you that "law is a jealous mistress"—usually without commenting on whether she is a satisfactory one. Or you may have a father or favorite uncle or family friend with a place in his office for you when you finish your studies, and this may be the determining factor in your choice. A few of you may have parents who will decide the matter for you on the assumption that they are better able to make the decision than you are. A few of you may come into law school to see whether you like it well enough to continue. Others may study law not because they intend to practice, but because they believe or have been told that it is a valuable background for business, public service, or politics.

If you are coming into law as the result of your own decision and not because your parents decided for you or because you are to inherit a practice, and if you intend to practice law, as the majority of law students do, then it is well to bear in mind certain questions as you approach a decision: Do I possess the qualities of mind and nature which are generally regarded as necessary to the profession? Do I see in the law an opportunity for real service? Do I believe that this service will permit me to use my talents in a way satisfying to me?

These are not easy questions to answer at any time. Particularly are they difficult at a time when you have had no experience in the matter about which you are deciding. For this reason, it has seemed best to talk for a while about the legal profession and lawyers. These remarks are in no way

intended as a substitute for talking over the matter with your
friends at the bar or your teachers.   They are merely intended to point the way for such discussions.   Before you
start on a journey, it is always well to know something of
the way ahead.   As a former teacher once told me, "half
of our time is wasted because we do not know which are the
important questions to be asked."

What Lawyers Do

There is little need here to remind you that law is an old
and honored profession and that it has numbered in its mem-
bership many of the leaders in thought and action.   This is
familiar knowledge gained from any history book.   But perhaps it would be well to tell you something of what lawyers
do.   In our society they perform many functions.   They
are the counsellors and advisers of men in matters of business, in family affairs, in government; in short, in whatever
realm of activity the law touches.   They are the protectors
of men's rights.   They are the planners for men in such
matters as the disposition of their estates during life and after
death, the employment of their funds, and the organization of
their personal and business ventures.   Lawyers are also
called upon to become judges and to assume the duty of interpreting and applying the law.   Lawyers are frequently
called upon to draft legislation or ordinances or the by-laws
which govern a corporation or society.   These are the general
functions of the lawyer.

However, as society has become more complicated and the
number of laws greater, lawyers, particularly in large cities,
have come to specialize in certain fields of legal work.   Thus,
some lawyers are known as "trial lawyers," because they
are primarily interested in presenting and arguing cases in
their initial appearance before courts.   Others specialize only

in cases which have been appealed to higher courts after the first trial. Some lawyers rarely go to court at all, preferring to confine their work to counselling and research, and so are known as "office lawyers." There is also a specialization in the type of legal matters handled. Everyone knows of the so-called "criminal lawyer" who is primarily interested in cases involving the commission of a crime. Or one hears of "tax lawyers," "corporation lawyers," "patent lawyers," or "labor relations counsellors." In recent times, we have begun to find some lawyers attempting to combine their legal knowledge with some other field of study—for example, law and engineering, law and accounting, law and medicine—in order to enable them to cope with complicated legal matters more intelligently. Thus law presents many facets, any one of which may challenge your special interest.

Do You Have the Qualifications?

One of the questions with which we said you ought to come to grips was that of whether you possess the qualities of mind and nature which are generally regarded as useful in the legal profession. Perhaps no two lawyers would agree on an exact statement of these qualities, but certain ones seem to stand out in any evaluation.

The lawyer should be interested in taking on and solving other people's problems. In large measure, the lawyer's stock-in-trade is his ability to solve satisfactorily problems which other people bring to him. When a man has a stomachache he goes to his doctor; when he has a spiritual problem he goes to his priest or minister; and when he has a legal problem he goes to his lawyer. For example, the man with the problem of providing for the disposition of his estate after his death so that his wife and children will be cared for; the man whose creditors are threatening to push him into bankruptcy; the man who wishes an agreement drawn up for the sale of his house at a certain price; the manufacturer who wishes to enter into a contract with his union employees or to issue new bonds or securities; the wife who desires a divorce from her husband; the man who has just been injured in a motorcar accident; the married couple who desire to adopt a child; the man who has just been accused of embezzling funds; all these are people who customarily turn to the lawyer in order that they may shift the burden to trained shoulders.

The lawyer must be able to accept that burden and the responsibility of doing all that he can to resolve the problem. This means that he must be interested in people and their problems and must desire to aid them to the best of his ability. The client is quick to know whether the lawyer is interested solely in the fee or in the client's problem, and when he has a problem which he considers sufficiently serious to require legal advice, he wants his adviser to treat the problem seriously.

By the same token, the client wants the lawyer to maintain an objective attitude toward the problem so that he can take clear-headed action. There are many people who can react to a problem in an emotional manner; sometimes these emotional reactions exceed even those of the man with the problem. This is not the quality sought in the lawyer. He is expected to remain cool, steady, objective, even detached, in order that he may bring to bear upon the problem all of his skill, reason, and experience. This does not mean that the good lawyer does not, like the good doctor, make the client's problem his own. He does; but he does so in order that he may understand the matter completely and so see how best to take action. This sense of calmness under fire, of cool thought, distinguishes the good lawyer as well as the good soldier. Some say that this trait comes only with long experience, but even so it is possible to recognize the beginnings of the trait at an early stage.

All of this does not mean that lawyers may not sometimes rap tables and engage in all the devices of histrionic rage and emotion. Some clients expect this as an indication of the lawyer's devotion to their case, but these emotional outbreaks are usually praised only in proportion to their ultimate effect upon the judge or jury in a particular case. They are not substitutes for coolly planned action.

Despite the fact that we have said that a lawyer should be interested in taking on and trying to solve other people's problems, it should be pointed out that the lawyer can deal only with such problems as are brought to him. However much he may wish to handle a particular matter, he cannot do so unless a client brings it to him and requests him to act. Even when the client brings a particular problem to the lawyer, it is still the client's problem. The lawyer's duty is to advise the client, to counsel with him as to his rights and duties, and to suggest to him a course of action. He guides the client in the law, but he cannot force the client to take the advice. As a lawyer, he may refuse to take the case at all. Further, if the client will not accept or follow his advice, the lawyer may withdraw from the case. There is no obligation upon the lawyer to carry out a client's wishes which the lawyer knows or believes to be illegal or unwise. Similarly, the client is not required to continue in the lawyer-client relationship if he believes that the lawyer is not adequately protecting his interests. The lawyer's skill is the vehicle through which the client's wishes may be made effective. It is a relationship of trust, freely entered into, in which the lawyer engages to act as the client's legal adviser and to assist the client in his lawful affairs.

The entertainment fields of the stage, films, radio, and television have quite naturally concentrated upon the dramatic side of the legal profession in the courtroom, and, again quite naturally, they have omitted from that limited portrayal all technical details unlikely to amuse or interest the patrons. Hence, before you accept the glamorized entertainment-world version of the lawyer's lot as definitive, go to your local court house and listen to a trial. Pick an ordinary day and not just the occasional murder trial. Put yourself in the place of the participants in this trial and see whether the prospect appeals to you. It is amazing how many law students have never heard an actual trial, and yet the whole experience is there for you to observe. Then, if the opportunity comes, visit an appellate court and watch the lawyers and judges in action there. This so-called "litigation" aspect of law practice is to many the most fascinating part of the business. Here is the excitement of actual argument and debate, and the satisfaction of having your argument accepted, if such is your lot.

Remember, however, that the trial phase of the lawyer's work is only a small percentage of his total activity. When you view a trial or go to hear an appeal, it is as if you came into the theatre to see the final polished version of a play. Behind this performance in court and in preparation for it have gone endless hours of research, investigation, writing, discarding, re-writing. There are the long hours of interviewing witnesses and examining documents. There is much digging in the old law books to find the law which applies to your client's case. A lawyer must of necessity do a great deal of reading and research. The old law resides in books filled with the opinions of judges, and it must be dug out as the miner digs, separating the dross from the gold. It is not as if the law had all been written out, so that, once it had been read, you would be done.   Each year thousands of new decisions are handed down and hundreds of volumes of them are printed, in the very center of which may be lurking the authority which the lawyer needs for his case.   It cannot be assumed that research is merely an incidental chore of "lawyering"; often it is the very core of the matter.   Hence a lawyer cannot afford to be a careless or indifferent reader, nor can he be one who is bored with research.   Perhaps in his later years he can retain junior lawyers to do his research for him, but at the outset of his career he will be the one to dig in the books, the statutes, and the journals.

With the older professions of law, medicine, and the Church has always gone a great sense of responsibility.   The lawyer, although he takes no such detailed oath as that of Hippocrates for the doctor, yet he assumes by virtue of his oath a solemn duty to his clients, to his fellow lawyers, to the court, and to the law itself.   Professional men take pride in this obligation and must be diligent in its observance.   As with the doctor, the lawyer is sometimes charged with the saving of a man's life.   Frequently, he is charged with the responsibility for managing his client's affairs and worldly goods—for example, when he sets up a trust fund, draws a will, or forms a business partnership or corporation.   The law is not a profession for one who shrinks from the assumption of responsibility.   Nor, and this is more important, is it a profession for one who feels no sense of obligation for the responsibility he has assumed.   The temptation to take advantage of one's position of trust is a real one, not to be considered lightly.   If you do not have the stamina to resist, do not put yourself in the way of the snare.

As one of the fruits of the full acceptance of this obligation of responsibility comes the sense of trust and confidence which other people feel in you.   This is extremely important to the lawyer because it is frequently necessary for the lawyer to be told details of his client's most intimate life or for him to be told of the inner workings of a man's business affairs.   Few people will tell these secrets to one whom they do not trust.   It is therefore necessary for the lawyer to be scrupulous in observing the confidential nature of these transactions and in all ways to merit the trust which the client places in him.   The man who talks too freely about matters which have been revealed to him in confidence will find that his clients will go elsewhere.   Similarly, if the client does not have confidence in the lawyer, he may withhold information, which in the long run may embarrass the lawyer as well as the client.

Thus far we have stressed the side of a lawyer's profession which touches his ability to understand and to work at solving other people's problems.   A great part of a lawyer's time is spent in the work of understanding and plotting a course of action.   But this is by no means all.   Having understood a problem and having decided on a course of action, he must communicate these ideas and these proposed actions to someone else.   For example, he must communicate them to his client, because, as we have said earlier, the lawyer can advise the client but it is the client who decides whether to act. Further, the lawyer must communicate these ideas to a judge or jury, if the matter goes to trial.   Thus it becomes important for you to ask yourself whether you have great difficulty in communicating your thoughts in speech or writing. By this is not meant whether you are ever at a loss for words or for the right word.   That is something which plagues us all at times.   We are even entitled to be lazy occasionally and say, "You know what I mean," just to save ourselves the trouble of spelling it all out.   However, there are some people who have a phobia about the blank sheet of paper or about writing, who cannot get their thoughts down, or who never seem to be able to say what they mean. The lawyer cannot afford such a phobia. There are also people who may be ever so brilliant at absorbing knowledge but who are unable to explain or pass on that knowledge to others either in writing or by the spoken word.

The faculty of communication is a subtle art. The complete lawyer needs it in all of its various forms. He must be able to draw up agreements which will express clearly and unmistakably the wishes of his client. He must be able to advise his client as to his rights in terms which the client can understand. He may be called upon to write the minutes of a meeting of a corporation or to draw up resolutions for the directors or shareholders. He must be able to convey precise images to the court in oral and written pleadings and briefs. Oratory may cover up a certain amount of loose thinking, but in the final analysis it is meaning expressed in simple terms which the lawyer wishes to convey to the court or jury. Facility in writing and speaking can be cultivated by practice and study. If your capacity be weak in this respect, you should give it careful attention.

Coupled with this faculty of communication of ideas to others is the further faculty of being able to listen attentively and intelligently so that you can receive ideas from others. Despite years of experience with the radio, we are not, as a nation, careful listeners. A foreign visitor once described American conversations as speeches delivered by each participant in turn without reference to what the other person had said. There is more than a morsel of truth in this observation. The lawyer, like the doctor, must be a good listener. He must listen carefully to all that his client says, automatically noting the statements which are relevant to the problem at hand, putting aside those clearly irrelevant, and placing in the middle those which may or may not be relevant. Or again he must listen carefully to all that a witness or an opposing lawyer says, because he can thereby detect the weaknesses in the argument or case made against him. You cannot do this by day-dreaming. The faculty of listening intelligently is unfortunately a rare one. Most people have to cultivate it. You can develop it by simple exercises. For example, listen to some speaker on the radio and attempt to remember certain facts or figures which he gives, or watch for inconsistencies in his statements, or count the number of times he uses a certain phrase, or outline his remarks. The same technique applied to classroom lectures frequently produces sound results.

There is also a little of Sherlock Holmes in every lawyer in his preoccupation with the "why" of things and events. You can see it at work in the lawyer's attempts to reconstruct the scene of a traffic accident or of a crime. Or it may be seen in the lawyer's efforts to understand the intention behind a certain act of the legislature or a written agreement or a last will and testament. The lawyer studies carefully each fact as if he were working on a giant jigsaw puzzle. Out of these facts he constructs a theory which he checks and rechecks against the known facts. Only when he has found a theory which takes reasonable account of the facts as he knows them does he feel certain that he has mastered the "why" of the case. The careful lawyer wishes to satisfy not only the "whys" which arise in his own mind but also those which he suspects his opposing counsel will discover. To many lawyers, this search for the "why" is the most exciting part of their profession.

Finally, our lawyer ought to possess a goodly measure of patience. Again, as a nation, we are not a patient people. We have always preferred action to waiting. Yet patience is a most valuable tool for the lawyer.   The patient man, on the whole, has a better chance to control the situation favorably than the frantic one.   By patience is not meant dilatoriness or do-nothingness.   Lawyers are sometimes accused of these things, but these are not what is meant.   Patience means waiting until the matter is ripe for action, until the quarry is squarely within the sights.   There are some things that man cannot hurry, and it is well to realize this at the outset.

You may at this point object that what we have been describing is the paragon of lawyers and that if you must possess all of these qualities law is not for you.   It is true that few people, except impossible braggarts, would be able to answer with a hearty "yes" to the possession of all these qualities.   This is not fatal.   The important thing is that you should know the direction in which you should proceed, not that you should arrive there before you start.   These are the marks and functions of the complete lawyer.   If you can see yourself as possessing or developing the majority of these qualities, then you can answer the first question which we have posed.   It was Chesterton, I believe, who made the seemingly paradoxical remark that if the thing is worth doing, it is worth doing badly.

We said earlier that in making your decision you should also bear in mind the question whether you see an opportunity for real service in the profession.   Actually this is a matter which you will keep under investigation all through your period of law study.   It breaks down into several factors: where you would like to live; where there is the greatest need for lawyers; and where the greatest opportunity exists for the kind of practice in which you wish to engage.   If you wish to practice in a small town, then you will canvass the areas you know to find one which has a need for additional lawyers and which is the kind of community in which you wish to live and bring up a family. It is frequently helpful if you can find an opening in your own home-town, where you and your family are already established and known. But lawyers must go where the legal business is found, and so it may be necessary for you to put down roots in a new community.

Those who wish to enter some form of government legal service will find that the areas in which they may be called on to work depend upon government expansion. Those who wish to specialize in fields of law such as admiralty, labor law, or corporation law will find it necessary to live in large industrial or port centers of population. Such considerations may be important in determining whether you prepare for law at all, but more likely they will be items kept in mind during your law study, to be decided when you have finished your studies, looked over the field, and estimated the chances for success and satisfaction in various places.

The Satisfactions of Law Practice

Many writers on professional guidance would not include the last question we have posed, namely, do you believe that this service will permit you to use your talents in a way satisfactory to you? Perhaps they shy away from it be-cause it is a personal matter. Perhaps they consider that it is so elementary as not to require mentioning. It does, how-ever, lie at the crux of the matter of personal choice, because effort expended in a direction which gives the actor no sense of personal satisfaction leads more often to ulcers and psy-chiatrists than it does to successful living.

This does not mean that every phase of the legal profession must be satisfying to you. Law, like other professions, has its routine tasks, its dull days. Rather this means that the ideals which lawyers strive to serve, the general outline of the functions which they perform in society, appeal to you as sound and good. So long as these things possess a challenge for you, call forth a desire to make yourself part of them, then you will not grow stale or find one day that you are in a rut from which all meaning has fled.

What then are some of the satisfactions which the law offers? From a material sense, although it does not produce as many millionaires as the oil industry or business, yet it has provided a comfortable living for most men. From a community point of view, the lawyer holds a respected position as long as he respects the position which he holds. The lawyer is expected to and does take part in community affairs which bring a sense of satisfaction to most men.

In a personal way, the lawyer finds satisfaction in the fact that he is dealing with people who have problems and need help and, in bringing to bear his own special talents, the lawyer feels that he is playing a useful part in his society. Then, too, most lawyers will tell you that there is great diversity in their work and that no two problems ever seem exactly alike. In order to approach the problems, it may be necessary for the lawyer to explore what are to him totally new fields of knowledge. One week he may become an "expert" on hydraulic pumps and the next on injuries to the eye. Then, too, the lawyer deals with his wits, with ideas and concepts, with experience and facts; and in the building of a good argument, the drafting of a sound instrument, the successful protection of his client's rights, there is a good feeling of accomplishment. There is also a pleasant sense of continuity in belonging to the profession of law, in being a part of an ever-developing effort to help men to live at peace with one another, to help to keep untangled the manifold interests and desires which men feel and fight for in society.

The choice of what to do with one's life is not an easy

one.   Nor are the considerations which go to back up the choice easy to satisfy.   There is much gratification in knowing that you have made a wise choice.   Therefore it is worth deliberating carefully over these things.   No one can choose for you in the true sense of that term; the choice and its responsibility are yours.   There is room for great service in the profession of law.   The challenge is still there for those who will take it up and respond with devotion.

3

"THREE TO MAKE READY"

What Background Is Necessary?

There are several avenues of preparation for the bar open to you, depending on the requirements of the state in which you wish to practice. Early in your thinking about law study, you should consult the specific regulations laid down by your state in this matter.

Some states still permit you to come to the bar by reading law for a prescribed number of years under the tutelage of a member of the bar. In the past, many of the leading members of the bar studied in this fashion. But at the present time it is customary to come to the bar only after a period of study leading to the degree of Bachelor of Laws. This law study is done either in a law school which forms part of a university or in a day or night law school having no connection with a university. In order to ensure the maintenance of proper standards and quality of instruction in these various law schools, the American Bar Association and the Association of American Law Schools have each established certain minimum standards which any law school must meet in order to be placed upon an accredited list. These law schools are periodically inspected and, if they meet these standards, they are given certificates to this effect. Under existing rules, credit which has been earned in a nonaccredited school is good only in that school and cannot be transferred as earned credit toward a degree in an accredited school.

Law schools, like those of medicine, being professional schools, are entered only after you have completed a certain amount of undergraduate college preparation. Admission requirements vary with different law schools, and hence the best advice is to get the catalogue of the law school which you desire to enter and set about to meet their stated requirements. Certain general remarks can however be made. The minimum time in which you can complete your undergraduate and law school studies is six years. During World War II it was possible in certain instances to expedite law studies and so finish in less time by going all the year around. Some universities divide this time into two years of undergraduate study and four years of law, while others follow the conventional pattern of three years of each. A few law schools require that applicants for admission possess a baccalaureate degree prior to entrance into law school. Many universities permit the law student to count his first year of law study as his senior year of undergraduate study and so permit him to receive both the undergraduate baccalaureate degree and the law degree in six years of study. It should also be pointed out that admission to law school study is not automatic. Many schools require, in addition to the minimum of hours of undergraduate study, the successful passing of legal-aptitude tests and the presentation of letters of recommendation, supplemented by personal interviews.

Undergraduate Study

There are two questions which crop up year after year in the counselling of prospective law students: Should I complete my undergraduate study for a degree before entering upon law study? What courses of study should I stress in undergraduate college as providing useful background material for law study?

Advisers are by no means in accord upon the answer to either of these questions. Some consider it the course of wisdom to say nothing about them. But there they are— two perfectly sound questions—and some beginning has to be made to answer them sometime. With this warning given, we can proceed to discuss them.

There are certain advantages to getting your degree before you enter upon law study. It enables you to complete and round out a full undergraduate program of planned study in your major and minor fields of interest. It brings you to law study somewhat older and with a successfully accomplished program behind you. Should you find after a year or so of law study that it does not interest you or that your law instructors do not find you sufficiently worthy to receive passing marks, or should you be forced to drop out for reasons of finance or military service, you leave the university with an earned degree. As we remarked earlier, some universities consider that one is ready for law study only after the successful completion of the work for an undergraduate degree.

Weighed against these advantages are the facts that the additional year or so of undergraduate study represents a considerable financial outlay and that it delays your entrance into practice. Perhaps the happiest compromise between the two positions is the so-called "combined degree program," which enables you to work toward both degrees concurrently by counting the first year of law study as satisfaction of the senior year of the undergraduate program.

In approaching this whole problem, it is well to remember that while there is an understandable desire to get on with one's chosen profession as soon as possible, yet it is also true that for most of us there does not come another chance in later years for formal education. Perhaps the best advice is to suggest that you get the best pre-legal education you can afford and as much as you can pay for.

When we turn to the question of what courses should be stressed in pre-legal education, it is exceedingly difficult to find agreement among the experts. For many years the law schools have debated the proposition whether to lay down hard and fast requirements for pre-legal education. Most law schools have shied away from laying down requirements and have confined their efforts to suggesting certain courses as valuable, either by means of notes in their catalogues or in personal interviews.

The truth of the matter is that law operates in such a wide area of activity as to make the whole catalogue of undergraduate courses useful to some extent. The fact that law schools do not lay down hard and fast requirements will not deter this or that law professor from remarking in class that if you had only taken a course in accounting in college, the problem at hand would be clearer for you, or from saying that if you had only learned your history properly you would not have made such a mistake, or from throwing up his hands in disgust and recalling his undergraduate days when (as he recalls now) English Composition required the writing of daily themes. One sometimes suspects that no law student ever came to law school with all the varied knowledge and background which his instructors expected him to have.

In the absence of agreement among the experts or stated requirements by the law schools, we have chosen to attempt to list some of those qualifications which law schools desire in their entering students rather than to list valuable courses. By concentrating on the development of these qualifications, we can at least know the direction which our studies should take. Actually, as will be seen, these qualifications should be the marks of any educated man.

Basic Skills

There are three basic skills which every law student needs: to read intelligently; to think logically and with an eye to experience; and to express himself clearly.

The beginning law student is set to work reading and digesting selected portions of the great storehouse of materials which have been written down by earlier judges, scholars, and legislators. For the man who can read intelligently and with discrimination, this reading brings him in touch with the dominant legal ideas of the centuries. To read intelligently means first of all that you understand the meaning of the legal terms used. Until your vocabulary has grown to the size of these varied writers, you will have to make steady use of a dictionary. This is particularly true in legal writings, since law has developed a vocabulary of its own, which must be mastered as soon as possible by the beginning student. Reading intelligently also means that the ideas presented must have meaning for you in order to enable you to follow the author's or the judge's line of thought. It means also that as you read, you should approach the matter critically, appraising the author's point of view, and, wherever possible, testing his statements against your own experience.

This skill in reading intelligently can be developed by your conscious efforts or as the by-product of almost any course in the university, wherein the instructor disciplines you to wring every ounce of meaning out of a page or sentence. It can be exercised not only in a foreign language course, where you must match meaning with meaning precisely, but also in a chemistry manual of instructions, where you must be able to follow given directions carefully. In law school there is much material to be read. Much of it is written in technical language. Students, perhaps rightly, feel that there is far more reading assigned than one can ever cover adequately. This means that law students can little afford to read the same page twice merely because they were not concentrating on the meaning the first time. They must learn to extract meaning with the least amount of wasted effort. Many universities have now set up "reading guidance clinics," in which you can test your reading power and set about to develop it to a higher degree of efficiency. These have proved especially helpful to pre-legal and pre-medical students. On the whole subject of reading intelligently, Professor Mortimer J. Adler of the University of Chicago has written a most useful volume entitled *How to Read a Book*.

The quality of thinking logically not only increases your appreciation and understanding of that which you read, but also helps to make effective the action you take. The man who reads many things and yet cannot arrange them in a coherent fashion travels with too many tag ends showing out of his luggage. At least since the time of the flowering of the common law in England, the study of law has been closely linked with logic. This has meant that succeeding generations of law students have been advised to study logic, which meant Aristotelian logic. When you come to study the opinions of the early judges and the intricate patterns of the rules by which a man's action was pleaded in the courts, you will see at work the practices and principles of logical thought.

The overzealous adherence to logic as the best guide to justice and reasonable decision was challenged by no less an authority than Mr. Justice Holmes when he wrote his famed generalization that "the life of the law has not been logic: it has been experience." Holmes saw the real growth of the law in terms of experience, and where the dictates of logic were in conflict with the knowledge gained through experience, then for him experience, rather than logic, became the guide to action.

Logic remains an important tool for the lawyer in approaching problems and in distinguishing adverse decisions, and the prospective law student will do well to develop the art of thinking in logical patterns.   This skill may be gained not only from formal courses in logic or semantics but also from any course in which the instructor is a disciplinarian in thought.   The social sciences, with their increased emphasis upon methodology, can also illustrate how logic and experience can exist side by side as useful approaches to understanding.

The third quality which you would do well to stress in your undergraduate study is the capacity to express yourself clearly.   This will stand you in good stead in classroom recitation, where your instructor will seek to discover the quality of your mind briefly and directly by the answers which you give to his questions.   The notion is very prevalent that the student who cannot express himself with reasonable clarity has failed to grasp the problem.   This quality is also useful in taking down notes in class based on the lecture or class discussion.   Since it is impossible to take down verbatim all that is said, unless you are a shorthand expert, you must be able to reduce to a few meaningful paragraphs that which has taken many, many words in the lecture or discussion. It is also important to possess the quality of clear expression in those inescapable examinations which dog a student's trail.   As many a sad student knows, no matter how much you have read or how much material you have cached away in your head, unless you can use that material effectively in writing answers to examinations questions, it avails you little for the purpose of getting through law school.   Unlike undergraduate courses, where frequent quizzes may help to supplement a poor performance on the final examination, it is usual in law school to have a single examination at the end of the course, which serves as the basis for your passing or failing the course. This puts great emphasis upon your ability to express your thought clearly in writing.

Training in expression can be accomplished. Whether you acquire this ability through writing freshman themes or in classes in advanced English Composition or through the preparation of laboratory reports and term papers does not matter. The important thing is that you acquire facility in writing and speaking. Courses in public speaking, particularly in extempore speaking, are valuable to the hesitant speaker. If the courses themselves do not give you sufficient experience, set yourself exercises, even if they be merely the improvement of the style and clarity of the letters which you write home. Whether one approves or not, the fact remains that many men have been saved from defeat by making unportant things sound important. A great actor can save a play which in lesser hands might justly reap bad reviews.

These then are the basic skills which you would do well to cultivate both in preparation for law study and in law school itself. You may well remark that in a sense they are basic to all learning. To these we would add three companion skills, which the law student will find of help in making the most of his legal training: a sense of history; the capacity to form value judgments; and the ability to formulate and recognize purpose and policy.

Supplementary Skills

A well-developed sense of history enables you to appreciate the full, continuous growth of legal ideas and problems. By this is meant an awareness that events do not occur in a vacuum, but should be studied against and as part of the background of the process of history. This sense of linking event with event, studying and comparing them against the "web of history" as the great Maitland called it, is of considerable value to the law student. In many law schools, there are courses in "legal history," in which the writings of such men as Maitland, Holdsworth, Vinogradoff, Holmes, Pound, and Woodbine are studied. It is a truism, but an often forgotten one, that "legal history" is but one facet of general history. From your courses in history, it is possible to get the feeling for the whole course of man's development, and to see that law, economics, the physical and social sciences, politics, and philosophy are all related parts of that stream. It is unfortunately true that one can take many courses in history without acquiring this sense. As long as history is thought of as simply a matter of dates or as events which happened a long time ago and then stopped happening, you cannot get a full sense of history. One can go through the motions of being a law student without this faculty but it is like viewing a scene in a black-and-white still photograph. The depth, color, and continuity are missing.

Or again, it is perhaps possible to go through law school without exercising your capacity to form independent value judgments, simply accepting as dogmatic truth those judgments which have been either written down by the author of the text from which you study or stressed by the instructor in the course. However, since it is your world as well as your neighbor's, you have the responsibility as well as the excitement of making independent value judgments. Law is sometimes distinguished from the physical sciences in that it deals frequently with judgments which defy precise measurement or prediction. Judges are required to choose between competing values which are urged upon them, for example, the weighing of a man's life against the protection of the peace of society, or the deprivation or restraint of a man's liberty when it is found that he is mentally incompetent. Lawyers and judges are both engaged in the adjustment of interests in the light of justice and fair play. This calls for responsible choice. In your studies in law school you will be called upon to comment upon past decisions of courts as to whether they are sound from the point of view of economic, social, or ethical values. You will be called upon to place yourself in the position of a judge and to evaluate competing arguments as to their relative value.

In bringing to bear this critical faculty upon your law studies you will come to feel a responsibility for law's growth and to appreciate its development in the hands of such judges as Mansfield, Marshall, Holmes, and Cardozo. For you must remember that the great events have not all happened, all the decisions have not been handed down, all the problems have not been solved. As law students and as lawyers, you will bear your share of responsibility for the wisdom of the decisions yet to be made.

It is difficult to say how one goes about gaining this experience and developing this faculty. Too frequently courses in ethics and value judgments become mere exercises in mechanics rather than applications to daily living. Those rare courses, under whatever name they are given, in which the student is encouraged or badgered into thinking for himself and in which the instructor dares to leave the text and to explore new fields or revisit old ones, are the courses which will help you to think for yourself. Thinking for yourself should not be confused with going against the stream of your fellows for the mere sake of novelty. You may well reach the same conclusions as your fellows but you will know why and how you got there, and in this knowledge you will have asserted your own integrity.

Growing out of this ability to form value judgments may well come a concern with recognizing and formulating purpose and policy. We sometimes forget that the ultimate purpose of all education is the deepening and enriching of the human spirit. We sometimes forget that when we study, we are studying about ourselves. We sometimes become so engrossed in our counting and labelling that we forget why it is that we count, why it is that we label. One of the great legal writers, von Jhering, has reminded us that "law is a means to an end," that it is not an end in itself. This century has seen an awakened interest among judges and lawmakers in the problem of the ends which law is to serve. Some writers and law schools have laid increased emphasis upon the lawyer's responsibility for the policy which the law pursues. This is part of man's seeking the "why" about all things, which leads him ultimately to a concern with the purpose of the universe in general and of man in particular. Whether this interest is expressed in the drafting of new legislative reforms or in an approach to an interpretation of the Constitution of the United States or the Charter of the United Nations, it presents a challenge to those who are prepared to take it.

Again, it must be admitted that were you to offer all these abilities to the dean of a law school as recommendations for admission to law study, he might well be either suspicious of your truthfulness or too amazed to react at all. These are the things which law schools wish that you had, but do not always expect to find. But again, they seem to be proper directions toward which to aim your pre-legal study. Remember that it is not the name of the course nor the text studied which makes it of value; rather, it is how much of the course becomes usefully integrated into you.

4

WHAT LAW IS ALL ABOUT

Scope of the Question

To ask what law is all about is a bit like the story of the lady who, finding that her dinner partner was a famous nuclear physicist and wishing to make him feel at ease, blandly asked him what all this fuss about atoms meant.

The nature of law is a simple enough question. Volumes have been written in an attempt to answer it. Historic feuds have taken place over the proper answer. If, in your first year of law study, you should chance to ask your instructor this question, he may quite probably tell you that it is an interesting question which should be held in abeyance until the third year. Others may give you what they call a "working definition." Still others may refer you to some outside readings in jurisprudence to be done in your spare time. A few may attempt to answer the question not by a pat definition but by explaining a few of their own impressions about law. They will try to answer it because it seems to them a proper and legitimate question on the first as well as the last day of law school. Perhaps even at the end of your career, you will still be attempting an answer. It is that kind of question.

It is somewhat as if we set out to study in detail all the characteristics and workings of the states of Massachusetts, Illinois, Wyoming, and Arizona and then were asked what the United States is all about. In our law studies we examine in considerable detail various aspects of the law, for example, the law of property, the law of contracts, the law of torts, the law of actions. We know as we study them that they are parts of the law but not the whole, that in many respects they are interrelated. We attempt to approach the whole by adding up the sum of all its parts. But in law as in the physical sciences, the whole is greater than the sum of all its parts.

The remarks which follow are set down because it is believed to be proper to ask the question "What is law all about?" and helpful to explore an answer. The answer will not be the same for all men, for in the end each man will have his own answer and in that answer will be revealed much of the character and purpose of the man who gives it. Since our space is limited, the answer must be exploratory rather than complete.

Law is About People

It is about the rights which people have in society. It is also about the duties which they have. It defines people's relationships to things and to other people. The laws of the physical sciences are about things or matter, but law, in the sense in which we use it here, is about people. This is one of the exciting things about law: we are not dealing with inanimate objects, but studying about men and women who can talk back and disagree. Every time you read a case reported in the law books, it is important to remember that the people named in the report are or were real people like ourselves, who considered the problem before them important enough to expend time, effort, and money in having it decided by a court. These people were not mere symbols *A* and *B* and *C*, although we frequently designate them so,

but they had names, desires, tempers, motives, and griev-
ances. It is also well to remember that the facts as reported
in the case were actual events and not "dreamed-up" situations; that the judge who sat at the trial and the lawyers who
argued the case were real people, subject to all the frailties
of human nature; that the jury which may be represented in
the report only by the words "verdict for defendant" was
composed of grocers and mechanics, bankers and business-
men, even as you know them in your own town.

Likewise, when you are reading the text of a statute or
city ordinance or a regulation of one of the government
agencies, it is useful to know that this is no pronouncement of
a Delphic oracle but a statement that was written, debated,
discussed, amended, and promulgated by men for themselves
and other men. To the extent that you can realize this fact
that law is about people and so project yourself into the discussion of events involving people of flesh and blood rather
than imaginary creatures, you will bring warmth and meaning to your studies and enthusiasm to your approach. The
practicing lawyer seldom forgets this fact. These people sit
in his outer office, are examined on the witness stand, com-
plain about or praise his efforts. He has little chance to
forget that they are real. The student, on the other hand,
who knows them only as meagerly described in the official reports, must make an effort to put flesh and bones around these
names.

Law and the Individual

The corollary of this notion that law is all about people
is the statement that law is all about us as individuals. Each
of us at birth possesses a body, drives and desires, and
capacities to satisfy these drives and desires. As we grow,
the objects of these desires change and multiply and our

capacities to satisfy these desires are increased. All of these desires and capacities go to make up what we may call our human personality. This personality does not depend upon law for its existence: it is, as the Declaration of Independence states, an endowment of the Creator. If a single man had the universe all to himself, there would be no need for him to make laws. However, since the individual man does not live in sole possession of the universe but shares it with others and since man's desires and capacities, unrestrained, can lead to the destruction of himself and other men, it has come about that men, acting together, have sought to impose and accept restrictions upon individual action for the common good. These restrictions and regulations become the rules, and these rules become the laws of any society.

Law is Man-made

This brings us to another remark as to what law is all about and that is that law is the man-made answer as to how the lives of men in this world are to be conducted. The importance of this statement lies in the assertion that law, as we consider it, is man-made. Law may recognize, protect, and regulate the activities of man's body, but law does not create man's body. Law must first have a created man upon which to operate. Every law which we have on our statute books, every regulation, every protected custom, every decision of a court, is the result of man's conscious activity. Even concepts, such as the right of self-defense, which are so ancient and hoary that their origins are shrouded in mystery, were originally established by men. Men, through law, have recognized the satisfaction of certain of the desires of men as worthy of legal protection, and we call these legal interests. Men, through law, have prohibited the satisfaction of certain of man's desires, and the doing of these acts has been termed unlawful action. Men, through law, have recognized that the gratification of certain of man's desires is worthy of protection only if carried out in a particular manner.

Let us take some simple examples. A man has the capacity to build a house on a certain plot of land which he alone possesses. The law has recognized the ownership of land and buildings as a protected legal interest and so will protect this man's interest against those who would seek to destroy his house. A man may have the capacity to take the life of another man, whose face annoys him, but the law has prohibited one man from taking another's life for such a reason. A man may have the capacity to sell poisons without labelling them as such, but the law has provided regulations which require such labelling. A man may have the desire for more than one wife at a time, but the laws of this country permit him to have only one, although men in some countries have decided that man's life is properly run with several wives if he so desires.

Human Personality and Legal Personality

From all this we get a concept of man's legal personality. His human personality is that which has been given by his Creator, while his legal personality is that which man through law recognizes and protects. Human personality does not depend upon law for its existence; legal personality does not exist apart from law. Thus law is all about man's legal personality. As an example, the birth of a child to a mother does not depend upon law; it occurs in the realm of human personality; but once the child is born it becomes vested by law with legal personality and has rights and duties as a son respecting its parents. In terms of legal personality, the child may be called legitimate or illegitimate; in terms of human personality, no such distinction exists. You will find, for example, that courts are divided on the question of whether a child in the womb of its mother can be said to have legal personality and be the possessor of rights and legal interests.

In understanding the distinction between man's human and legal personality, we find, for example, that man possesses desires and capacities which are not protected or given effect to in law.   There is no human impossibility in an insane person's or an infant's going through the motions of agreeing to buy or sell land, yet the law will not grant enforcement to such a bargain and hence the transaction does not result in a change in legal personality.   Or again, for many years people in private life desired to be let alone to live privately and not to have their faces and lives spread over the public press and frequently they engaged in measures of self-help to prevent such being done.   However, it was not until the latter part of the last century that the men who make the law decided to give protection to this desire as a valid legal interest, now usually referred to as the "right of privacy." We have seen in our own country the granting of rights to married women which could be exercised by them in their own legal capacity.   The history of law is filled with examples showing that many desires and capacities which men have long possessed have gradually become recognized as legal interests.   Whenever you hear the expression "there ought to be a law about it," you are witnessing the fact that law has not yet encompassed all of human activity.

It is also true that in some instances a man's legal personality is greater than his human personality.   For example, we have provided laws whereby a man's desire as to the disposition of his property after death may be given effect, even after he has died.   The man, being dead, no longer has the human power or capacity to effect this distribution, but it is accomplished by laws giving effect to his will or testament. Similarly, the law affords protection to a man's property and contract rights even after he has lost the capacity to act for himself, such as when he is insane. Or again, a weak man may not be able to take physical vengeance upon another who has injured him, but the law, protecting his legal right to be free from wrongful harm, may come to his aid and enforce compensation or mete out punishment to the wrongdoer.

There are some instances in which, through law, men have attributed personality where none exists on the human level. The prime example is the state, which is treated as a person in law, capable of making contracts, committing wrongs, and of suing in the courts. No one has ever seen or pretends to expect to see that state as a human person. All know that states can only act through people and yet we accept easily the notion of personifying the state. It is created by law and given the attributes of personality by operation of law. Similarly, the business corporation, which bulks so large in importance in our economic life, is regarded in law as a separate person from its members and agents, although again no one has ever seen a corporation in the flesh. This is not to deny the utility of these fictions which men have seen fit to set up. It is only to point out that the fiction becomes and remains "real" only so long as the cloak of legal personality protects it.

Purpose of the Law

Thus far we have said that law is about people, and that law is man-made. We have seen that the raw material upon which law operates is man as a human being. Thus you have, on the one hand, man as a going concern, already created, and, on the other hand, the laws which man has created for himself. We can assume that the forces which drove man to establish laws were self-interest and self-preservation. As students, you will study the laws which man has made, their application, and their interpretation. You will note that man's laws are not the same in all countries nor even in all parts of the same country. You will learn, for example that in some places a father may disinherit a son and cut him off "without a shilling," while in other places he may not do so. You will learn that a man may contract a marriage or get a divorce in one state by forms and on grounds which would not be valid in another state. For some of you it may seem enough to learn these differences; others may be stirred to seek for the reasons behind the differences. This has been so with men from the beginning.

This speculation about law is sometimes called "jurisprudence" and sometimes "legal theory" or "legal philosophy." These speculators, in seeking to discover what law is all about, at some time or other pose for themselves the question as to whether man's law has any central purpose, any integrating plan. Here one finds two extreme views. The one maintains that man's laws have grown up in response to felt needs, rules being made only for immediate problems without any attempt to follow or prescribe in advance any general principles or set plan. Advocates of this view point to the fact that cases are decided by courts on particular points of law between particular persons and become law only on that point, and that statutes are usually passed to remedy specific evils or to provide for specific problems.

The other view holds that the creation of laws by man has followed and is following a definite plan or purpose; that laws are created not merely as pragmatic solutions to specific problems but consciously in the fulfilment or unfolding of a general plan or set of major principles. It is sometimes said too glibly that the former position more accurately describes the Anglo-American common law, while the latter describes the point of view of the civil law which prevails on the European continent and in Latin America.

As is frequently the case where two extreme positions are stated, neither one encloses the whole truth, although each bears a part of it. Certainly you can find that much in the law you will study appears to have been devised to meet specific problems. But you will also find instances in which judges and legislators appear to be stating and following certain general principles. Without going into greater detail, perhaps enough has been said to indicate that part of the question of what law is all about involves the larger question of what man is all about. The legal philosophers and theorists no less than their counterparts in general philosophy have long debated and will continue to debate the answers to these questions. You, too, will have your chance to enter the debate.

Expansion of Law

There is one further remark which should be made concerning what law is all about. Man, through law, is dealing with ever-increasing areas of activity. This is shown not only in the great increase in laws and regulations but in the fact that men everywhere are feeling the effect of laws which they make. Areas of activity which previously were left to individual action free from specific regulations, such as labor relations, insurance, and the issuance of securities, are now included within the reach of the law's regulatory hand. Whereas formerly laws were thought to be in many respects the special interest of the rich and powerful, now laws reach every citizen, whether it be in matters of income taxation, social security, or agricultural planting. Hence more people than ever before are interested in what the law is all about. The dictates of law are being questioned and tested in many new ways. As long as law was considered to be divine in origin or the perfection of reason and logic, its pronouncements could be challenged only on grounds of scripture, divine revelation, or logic. But as law has come to be thought of as grounded not solely in divine inspiration, immutable principles, immemorial custom, and logic, but also in experience, it has followed that law's dictates have been challenged by those who have made that "experience" their special study.

For example, the law sets forth certain tests for the determination of insanity. These tests are being challenged by many psychiatrists, who consider knowledge about insanity to be their special bailiwick. The law sets forth certain regulations in the interest of small business. Some economists claim that the law will not produce benefits to the small businessman. The law sets forth certain grounds upon proof of which a divorce may be granted, but denies a divorce on other grounds. Experts in family relations attack the wisdom of these laws in certain particulars. The law sets forth methods of business accounting for corporations. Certain accountants term these methods obsolete. The law's theory of punishment has drawn prolonged debate from sociologists and criminologists.

The truth of the matter is that law is coming to be about more and more of man's activities, not only in general outline but in specific details. Law has come into the market place, where formerly other disciplines held undisputed sway, so that the lawyer finds himself dealing not only with the old traditional law materials but also with the concepts of the economist, the sociologist, and the psychiatrist. The world of "lawyering" in which you enter is a more exciting but also a more complex one than that in which your father would have entered.

Some of these comments may indicate why it is so difficult to answer the simple question of what law is all about. Once it may have been easier, but now certainly it is mixed up with "sailing ships and sealing wax and cabbages and kings."

5

CURRICULUM—CURRICULA

Classification of Law

Ever since man got the notion of dividing and classifying, he has spent a considerable portion of his time and effort in breaking things up, giving to the parts names, and arranging them in patterns. Now and then, he has spent some time in putting them back together again.

Law has shown little tendency to be free from this popular pastime. The old Romans under the Emperor Justinian set about to place the many scattered pieces of their law into some order, and the famous Code, Digest, and Institutes which resulted from their efforts have had a marked influence upon the law classifiers ever since. The Romans followed roughly a threefold division: the law of persons, the law of things, and the law of actions. Many countries which follow the civil law tradition still use this basic division, with some variations.

In the common law, which England developed and the states of the United States, except Louisiana, received as their basic law, Sir William Blackstone was an outstanding systematizer. When Sir William was appointed as the first holder of the Vinerian Professorship of English Law at Oxford in 1758, he took as his first task the reduction of the scattered bits of English case law, statutory law, and customs to some order so that he could lecture on this law in an understandable, coherent fashion. These lectures later became the basis of his famous work *Commentaries on the Law of England* which had a great effect upon American law in its formative period.

Following the revolution in France, efforts were made there to fuse together into a code the written law (*droit écrit*) and the customary law (*coutumes*) as practiced in France, cleared and purged of old feudal notions and extended and interpreted by eminent French jurists. The result was the famed *Code Napoléon,* which served as a model for many other countries. At the turn of the century, the German Civil Code, hailed by some as "more scientific" than the French, was completed and became a rival model to that of France. In the United States during recent years we find the American Law Institute engaged in the monumental work of restating the law as applied in this country in such fields as contracts, tort, property, agency, and trusts.

Division of Law into Courses

One aim of all these projects has been to overcome some of the uncertainty and confusion as to what the law is, by placing it in such a form and arrangement that it can be found more easily and studied more meaningfully. Schools of law, faced by the task of instructing men in the rudiments of law in the brief period of three years, have also sought to achieve patterns and divisions in law which will render it more easily learned and taught. Law schools in civil law countries, having their law in codified form, can base their instruction upon the general divisions of the codes themselves. However, in common-law countries, such as the United States, where there are few formal codes and where each of the states is engaged in developing its own law, law schools have taken as the common denominator for teaching purposes a division of law into courses.   Thus you find in the modern law school that law is taught in the form of such courses as contracts, tort, real property, or taxation.   <u>Within each course are gathered and taught the relevant court decisions, statutes, administrative rulings, and leading theories pertaining to that field of law</u>.

You will also discover that these courses are offered in some sort of sequence or hierarchy.   This too is done for educational purposes based on both the complexity of the course and the relationship of the courses to one another. For example, one course may build upon concepts previously learned in another course.   Law schools are continually studying their curricula, occasionally dropping out old courses or consolidating them with others, adding new courses, and engaging in new experiments.   But despite variations found from school to school, there is enough standardization in modern law schools to permit general comment upon these divisions.

In the typical law school, during your first year of study you will be introduced in fairly thorough fashion to the basic themes of law.   You will study the law of contracts, dealing with the voluntary agreements into which a man can enter, how they are made, and how they are enforced.   You will also study the law of tort, sometimes called obligations imposed by law as distinguished from contracts or voluntary obligations, in which you will deal with wrongs done to a man for which he seeks relief, usually in the form of damages. You will also study the basic property interests, and concepts of possession and ownership of things, whether they be land, buildings, stoves, horses, or shares of stock.   You will also be introduced in a preliminary way to the law of actions or procedure, wherein you will study the remedies available and the mechanics of a law suit.   You will probably have a course in legal bibliography in which you will learn to find and use the law books and to do exercises in legal research.   You may also study the law of crimes, concerning the punishment by the state of those found guilty of unlawful actions.   There may be other courses in your first year, but these are the basic themes.

It cannot be said too early or too often that the first year is the most important year of law study.   There is an old law school adage that the first year they scare you to death; the second year they work you to death; and the third year they bore you to death.   Be that as it may, a sound foundation must be laid that first year, because unless you have the themes well in mind you may soon be lost among the variations which come later.   As in music, if the themes are well grasped, the variations lose much of their difficulty and become more interesting.   In recognition of the importance of the first year, law schools look carefully at your first-year record as an indicator of whether you should be permitted to continue with law study.

During your second and third year you will study variations upon the theme of contracts, such as sales, negotiable instruments, and insurance, and you will also take up the counterpart of contracts, the law of bankruptcy, dealing with those who cannot satisfy their obligations.   You will study many variations upon the theme of property, such as mortgages, trusts, wills, gifts, estate planning, security rights, and the transferring of estates in land.   You will also find variations on the theme of remedies and procedure, such as the procedure of your own state, jurisdiction and procedure in the federal courts, equity, and perhaps advanced criminal law administration, as well as courses in evidence or proof. You will be instructed in the law of persons, both of natural persons in such matters as marriage, divorce and adoption, and of artificial persons such as corporations. You will be introduced to the field of public law, through such courses as constitutional law, administrative law, trade regulation, and international law. You will also meet that great synthesizer of all courses, conflict of laws or, as it is sometimes called, private international law. Finally, you may meet some of the new courses such as taxation, corporate finance, legal accounting, and labor law. There may also be seminars or discussion groups in jurisprudence, legal history, and comparative law.

During your first year you will not be troubled by the question of what courses to take, because in most law schools the courses to be taken by first-year students are prescribed. But in the second and third years a large amount of freedom of choice is normally permitted. Certain law schools go beyond the first year in requiring courses. A glance at the catalogue of your chosen law school will advise you as to which areas of choice are open and which are closed. Since in most law schools more courses are offered than you have time to take, your choice among the electives should be made with certain ideas in mind. Is this a course in which I have a particular interest or bent? Is this a course upon which I will be examined by the bar examiners of my state? Is this a course which is likely to prove useful in the practice which I hope to have? Is the instructor in this course one of those who give me good training in thinking regardless of the name of the courses which they teach? Upon this whole matter of selecting courses, it is well to take advice from your counsellor on the faculty or from your friends at the bar.

Limitations of the Curriculum

In spite of the merits of the system of breaking law up into courses for educational purposes, there is also some danger. In actual life it is seldom that a client comes in and says to you, "I have a problem in contracts." Rather he comes in and tells you certain facts as he sees them; it is up to you to decide whether it is a contract problem or not. Similarly, practice does not often present you with problems which lie solely in one field. You are likely to meet problems involving mixtures of several fields. Hence, it is well for you to keep in mind that the division into courses, though useful educationally, is artificial. You will learn the various parts of law, but you must do the putting together into a whole. Then, too, in examinations in law school the instructor will set questions regarding his own course. Thus, part of your work is already done for you, namely, selecting the field in which the problem falls. But bar examiners frequently do not label their problems but leave it up to you to decide what field the questions concern.

Therefore, although you receive your legal education in packets of courses, you must be on guard to see the wider limits of all law, the interrelation of its parts, and their points of difference. For example, in a case involving the sale of adulterated food in a restaurant your instructor in sales, reasoning from the law of contracts, may reach one result while your instructor in tort, applying the principles of established case law, may reach a contrary result, and your instructor in procedure and proof may indicate still further doubts as to the solution to be obtained in litigation.

In concluding this discussion of the courses in the typical law school, it is well to mention one further fact which, although self-evident, frequently causes dissatisfaction among new-born lawyers.   No matter how many courses are added to the curriculum or how much longer the period of instruction is extended, <u>all law is not and cannot be taught in law school</u>.   Even were it desirable to do so, it would be impossible to prepare you for all the problems which may arise to plague or intrigue you in the course of your career at the bar.   Most beginning lawyers will tell you that for a considerable time after they entered practice, they felt as "green as a freshman," as if they had learned nothing in law school. This will perhaps always be true despite the introduction in some laws schools of practice clinics.

During your law school study, you will be taught the fundamentals selected on the basis of long experience and such variations on the fundamentals as will give you a fair sampling of the usual problems.   You will acquire the major tools, methods, and techniques which mark the profession of the lawyer, but skill in their use is left to be developed in practice.   <u>The rest of your life will be spent in learning the law and in using it, and, even then, if you are at all normal, you will only scratch the surface of the whole.</u>

6

COURTS, JUDGES, AND JURIES

Your lives as law students will be intimately bound up with the doings of courts, judges, and juries, because the decisions of courts are in our society a leading source of law. In the formative period of the common law, the decisions of the judges as to the law of England sometimes outweighed the words of the Parliament. To some, the phrase "common law" meant the case law, the decisions of courts, while the statutes passed by the legislative body were thought of as rents in the fabric of the common law and so were construed strictly, lest they spoil the fabric. As we use the term "common law" in this country, it usually refers to that law which we took from England in the form of statutes as well as in the form of decisions of courts.

The importance of the rôle which courts play in our society is indicated by the fact that through the Constitution of the United States and the constitutions of each of the states, the people have entrusted to the judiciary the power to decide cases and controversies arising at law or in equity. The theory behind this is that judges, specially chosen and specially trained in law and equity, are best equipped to perform the function of deciding disputes arising among their fellow men. The power to hear and decide these cases is present only when the particular judge or court can be said to have jurisdiction by the law creating the court. It is the power or authority to speak or decide which makes a man or group of men into a court; absent this power and they remain merely men and in theory their decisions do not constitute law.

Federal Courts

In the United States there are two systems of courts: the federal system of courts sanctioned by the Federal Constitution and provided for by federal statutes, and the state and local courts sanctioned and provided for by the constitutions and laws of the various states. The highest court in the United States is the Supreme Court of the United States, established by the Constitution, consisting of nine justices appointed by the President with the approval of the Senate. One of their number is designated as the Chief Justice of the court. This court sits in Washington and has jurisdiction to hear certain cases as a court of first instance and, under certain designated circumstances, to review decisions of other federal courts and the decisions of the highest courts of the states and territories.

Because this court has the power to hear and decide cases which involve the construction of the Constitution and statutes of the United States, it is sometimes said that in our system of government the judiciary is supreme. That is, it can set at naught acts of the Congress or the President which it deems to be beyond the powers conferred by the Constitution upon these branches of government. This is popularly referred to as the "doctrine of judicial supremacy," the operation of which has sometimes irritated both Congress and the Chief Executive.

Below the Supreme Court in the hierarchy of federal judicial power are the ten courts of appeals and the court of appeals for the District of Columbia. The appellate jurisdiction of these courts is over matters arising in designated areas. These courts consist of from three to eight judges, depending upon the size of the particular circuit and the work to be done there, and they sit at designated places within the circuit. Below these courts are the district courts, of which each state has at least one. The distribution of these federal district courts depends upon the needs of the area, and the number of judges in such courts varies from place to place. In addition to these courts, there also exist in the federal system trial courts for the District of Columbia and for various possessions and territories, the Court of Claims (which has jurisdiction over certain claims made against the United States), the Court of Custom and Patent Appeals, the Tax Court, and the Court of Military Appeals.

State Courts

Turning to the state courts, we find that each state has its own system of courts, usually provided for by the state constitutions and in most instances modelled to some degree upon the English court system. Despite variations from state to state, certain general features can be noted. The final appellate tribunal of a state is normally called the Supreme Court, although, for example, in New York it is called the Court of Appeals and in Maine and Massachusetts the Supreme Judicial Court. The work of such courts is usually to hear and decide appeals, but in some instances they may also serve as trial courts. Below this court in the hierarchy are one or more appellate courts, the number depending upon the size and population of the state and their jurisdiction depending upon state statute. Below these courts we have the principal trial courts, usually established on a district or county basis, and the so-called inferior trial courts established on a city or township basis. In some states you will find separate courts

for law and equity, and in many states you will find separate
courts for special matters, such as probate courts and juvenile
courts.   This by no means exhausts the possibilities of listing,
but it is enough for illustration purposes.

As you come to study the court system of your own state,
you will discover that the power of each court is usually set
out by statute.   Courts created in one state are without power
in another state except as that other state may give effect to
their judgments or process.   It should also be noted that
within the various states sit both state and federal courts,
each deciding cases within its special competence.   Sometimes it happens that the procedure followed by the state and
federal courts differs in important details, so that it may be
to the advantage of the litigant to choose one over the other.
The rules which have been worked out for the harmonization
of the two systems, state and federal, so that conflict is reduced
to a minimum, will be discussed in your course in federal
jurisdiction and present some of the most interesting pages
of our legal history.

Judges

Whether we are discussing state or federal courts, it is
well to remember that courts are manned by judges and that
a court is as strong as the men who sit on it.   In a very real
sense, the choice of a judge in our system is more important
than the choice of a legislator or executive, because the judge
has in his hands the lives and property of men when these
matters are in dispute.   Therefore, in a democracy such as
ours, the manner in which these judges are chosen is a matter of importance.   In the federal system of courts, the judges
are appointed by the President with the consent of the Senate.
This means that the President's list of appointees is sent to
the Senate for confirmation.   These appointments are tradi-

tionally made from the ranks of practicing lawyers, but occasionally a judge is chosen who has also served as a law professor.

The methods used in selecting judges of state courts vary from the method of appointment to that of election by the people. There are staunch advocates of each method. The terms are fairly long, and the judge is usually eligible for re-election.

The judge performs many functions. <u>His prime duty is presiding over his court and seeing to it that each litigant gets a fair hearing and a just decision.</u> Within his court, he is the supreme master. He can cite for contempt those who in any way seek to prejudice or disrupt the orderly and seemly despatch of business. He can order people to appear in his court at stated times and can punish those who refuse to do so. <u>His less formal work is conducted "in chambers."</u> He acts as the supervisor of trustees or guardians administering funds which have been placed in the custody of the court and of administrators and executors of wills and estates. It is a position of the highest trust and responsibility, and just as we have said that a court is no stronger than those who sit on it, so too the laws themselves are adequate protection to men only when they are in the hands of able and trustworthy judges.

Juries

There is a further institution in our judicial system which merits some explanation. This is the jury. Let us take a simple thesis: we say that the judge applies the law, as he knows it or finds it, to the facts of each individual case as they appear or are found to be. We say that the judge is entrusted with the application of the law because he is learned in the law and is advised by lawyers who are likewise learned in the law.   But when we turn to the finding of the facts, deciding what actually happened in the controversy in which different versions of the event are offered by witnesses, we find two methods in use.   One of these is for the judge who hears the witnesses to find the facts.   This is what we call a trial to the court sitting without a jury.   The other method is for a jury of laymen to listen to the witnesses, look at the documents and exhibits, and find the facts acting as a body.   This we call trial by jury.

To keep our thinking clear, we must note that there are several kinds of juries.   <u>There is the so-called "grand jury," which sits as a body to hear evidence of alleged criminal acts,</u> this evidence being presented to it by the public prosecutor or district attorney, and to decide whether the persons involved in the acts shall be indicted and tried for the crime described in the prosecutor's bill.   Since a criminal action is brought in the name of the community, the grand jury represents the people in determining whether, upon the evidence, the people should take action against the one suspected of crime.

There are also the so-called "petit juries."   In a criminal trial it is customary to have a trial by jury, and the jury, having heard the evidence, observed the witnesses as they testified, and seen the exhibits, is then instructed by the judge as to the law of the case, and then retires into secret session to determine by discussion and ballot whether or not the accused has been proved guilty of the charge levied against him.   Hence, in a criminal trial the jury performs a very important function and bears a heavy responsibility.   <u>Juries are also used in civil cases, but it is frequently true that in civil cases the right to trial by jury is waived by the parties.</u>   Finally, it is to be noted that so important was this right of trial by jury held to be that a guarantee of it was incorporated into the Federal Constitution.

The idea of jury trial is deeply rooted in the history of English law as one of the bulwarks of man's freedom from tyranny. In its history and use, the concept of the jury has gone through many changes in form, but the fundamental idea remains that each man has the right to be tried by his fellow citizens. In its early form, it is likely that the jurors (the name taken from the Latin word for oath) were the neighbors of the persons involved in the controversy. Apparently, it did not matter that they already knew a great deal about the situation to be tried. In the modern form, the jurors are chosen from lists prepared of the eligible residents of the community in which the case is to be tried. Certain persons, such as lawyers, are exempt from jury duty. Others may be excused on grounds such as relationship to the parties or prejudice. Because of the importance of the jury in the trial, it is usual to permit the lawyers to challenge a given number of the prospective jurors as to their fitness to serve, lest prejudice to the parties result.

The modern idea is apparently to get a jury which knows as little as possible about the facts beforehand and which gives the minimum amount of evidence of prejudice. To this jury the proofs are presented, the exhibits are shown, and the pleas are made. In order to secure the jury's freedom from improper influence or prejudice, it is kept segregated as a body during the trial, and only designated persons have access to it. The proofs which are presented must be in a certain form and are subject to the scrutiny and objection of the judge and the lawyers. The whole procedure for trial by jury is carefully hemmed round with safeguards, which you will learn in your courses in evidence and procedure. In fact, it is sometimes said that much of the complexity of the law of evidence comes from the repeated attempts made by succeeding generations of lawyers to find ways and means of getting proof before the jury.

The physical scientists are impatient and critical of the judicial method of ascertaining fact. They point out that in many instances it is unscientific and sometimes patently absurd. They point out that in this area of legal endeavor, logic has run riot and conquered experience. But until some better method comes along and is proved, the lawyers point out that by and large this system produces sound results.

There is much more which could be said about judges and juries, but the present purpose is merely to introduce you to them as important factors in the process of making what we call case law. Case law in the Anglo-American legal system is of far more importance than it is in the civil law system which prevails in Europe and Latin America. This arises from the fact that in the Anglo-American system a point of law once decided by a competent court becomes a precedent binding upon lower courts in succeeding cases of like nature and can only be overturned by the same court or a higher court. The operation of this concept we call *stare decisis*, which, roughly translated, means to abide by or adhere to decided cases.

Thus in our system the rôle of the judge is a very important one, and courts exercise great power. The judge is controlled by the oath he takes to the people he serves, in which he swears to uphold and defend the constitution and laws of his country. Hence, we are accustomed to say that ours is a government of laws, not of men. This statement, roundly challenged by those who object to the personification of laws and the ignoring of man's frailties and foibles, remains a powerful and revered statement of our aims.

7

LEGISLATORS, EXECUTIVES, AND BUREAUS

The Legislature as a Source of Law

When most people think of law-making, they think of legislatures, where duly elected representatives of the people debate and pass statutes, resolutions, and codes. The Revolutionary War cry of "no taxation without representation" illustrated our firm belief that the people, who were subject to laws, should have a voice in their making. Hence, having just spoken of the decisions of courts as sources of laws in our system, we can now turn to the legislatures as sources of law.

To the student of civil law, as it prevails in Europe and Latin America, the prime source of law is the legislature, and he will study diligently the codes of law which have been passed covering the whole field of private civil law, procedure, crimes, commerce, and public law. The decisions of courts are to him secondary, since, as one of the civil codes states, "law is the solemn expression of legislative will." The legislative will, as expressed in the codes, serves as the guide or standard for the court, and when the judge has before him a case for which the code has no provision, then, for example, the Swiss Code instructs the judge that he is to act as if he were a legislator providing a law for that case.

In the Anglo-American system, as we have seen, the judge

and the legislator, each within defined areas, make law. It is sometimes said that, in the course of our early legal history, legislatures have acted to make laws only when the evil or problem was so great as to demand a remedy which the courts were unable or had been unwilling to give; or where the solution reached by the courts was at variance with the desire of the people as made effective through the legislators; or where the problem was new and required a new remedy which the legislature was willing to give. If one were to hazard a theory, it would seem that <u>in the main our legislatures have been content to allow courts to meet problems as they arose, with such tools and concepts as the courts had, or, on occasion, invented, reserving to the legislatures the right to enter into the matter by statute whenever the problem became so acute as to demand their attention.</u> Such a statement is of course oversimplified, but it contains the notion of the relationship of court and legislature which prevailed over much of our history. As long as strong and able judges were capable of extending and applying the old law to new situations as they arose, and as long as pressure from the people did not build up against such decisions, the system operated admirably.

<u>Within recent times it would seem that this trend has been reversed.</u> Problems which arose in the path of the industrial revolution, with its factory system and growth of large cities; complications and dangers presented by the use and development of the machine in all its forms; the awakened need for social reforms; the widespread economic depression of the early thirties; the impact of mobilization for two world wars; all these have presented tasks of adjustment which were too far-reaching and complex for courts to meet by the old legal forms, however skilfully handled. Pressures built up behind legislators for reform, for far-reaching legislation to cover and control these new problems.

Thus we have seen legislation in increasing amounts coming from our law making bodies, state and federal, covering such diverse matters as income taxation, motor vehicle operation, social security, and crop rotation. Whereas in a sense it might be said that the older legislation was directed toward the control of a problem, already developed and out of control, the new legislation is also concerned with prospective planning and regulation of whole areas of economic and social activity. Thus we are beginning to find modern legislation covering a whole field of action rather than comprising only piecemeal attack upon single problems. This development is by no means confined to the United States, but is apparent in other traditionally common law countries as well.

Courts and Statutory Law

If one is to judge by looking at the modern law reports, it would seem that present day courts are mainly concerned with the interpretation and application of statutory law, whereas formerly most of their work lay in the development and application of common law principles and decisions. This in turn has meant that courts, in applying statutes to individual controversies, have been concerned with two major questions. First, did the legislature possess the authority under the Constitution to legislate in that field? This is the famed argument of "unconstitutionality" on the basis of which so much was said and written in the thirties about the so-called "New Deal" statutes. In the record of that conflict between the Supreme Court of the United States, President Roosevelt, and the Congress are found some of the most interesting writings on constitutional government. Second, what is the meaning or intention of the statute in question?

Someone has said that he did not care who wrote the laws as long as he retained the power to interpret and apply them. Courts, in the last analysis, decide in disputed cases the meaning attached to the words of a statute; and since, even in the most semantically minded circles, words seem capable of various meanings at various times, courts have retained a decided measure of control through the power of interpretation, regardless of increased legislative activity. If you look at some of the modern statutes, you will discover that they frequently contain sections on "definitions" and "declarations of policy." These are placed there as a guide not only for those who execute the law, but also for courts which apply and interpret the law. In order to ensure that full effect will be given to the legislative intention, legislators have paid greater attention to the technicalities of drafting legislation; and over a long period of time, courts have come to follow certain canons of construction announced in individual cases. You will undoubtedly hear much in law school about the question of whether some judges have allowed their economic and social theories to affect their choice among competing meanings of legislative words and phrases.

Executive Law

The executive branch of the government is also a source of law—for example, through orders issued under executive authority. In times of war and emergency, the executive authority is increased, its exact limits still being subject to heated debate. The power of the President as head of the state in foreign affairs is likewise an area into which we have only begun to explore. These are matters which you will touch upon in your courses in constitutional law and public international law.

Administrative Agencies

Within the past seventy-five years there has developed in this country a further source of law, in the rules, decisions, and regulations of administrative agencies or bureaus. There are those who consider these as an infernal bureaucracy of red tape, while others point out that they are a reasonable response to a pressing need for economic and social regulation. Debate still continues as to whether they should be considered as an unauthorized "fourth branch" of the government or as a functional integration of the three traditional branches. At all events and without our getting into this controversy, the fact remains that these agencies do make rules and regulations and hand down decisions and orders, thus performing legislative, judicial, and executive functions of some order. Examples of the many such agencies on the federal level are the Interstate Commerce Commission, the Federal Communications Commission, the National Labor Relations Board, the Civil Aeronautics Authority, and the Atomic Energy Commission.

These boards or commissions are normally created by legislative act and are entrusted by the legislature with the administration of designated statutes. For example, the Congress established the Securities and Exchange Commission in 1934 and charged it with the administration of the Securities Act of 1933 and the Securities and Exchange Act of 1934. Since that time, the administration of several other acts has been turned over to the Commission. This has meant that the Commission would take the general standards laid down in the acts, spell them out into specific rules and regulations, and require compliance with these rules. In the event of disputes, the Commission would hear and decide such disputes, subject to having its decision reviewed by the courts. From a practical point of view, these agencies have become a very powerful factor in government. Their many rulings and regulations have made the present-day lawyer's task of searching out the applicable law a far more difficult one than that which his colleague of some years ago had to undertake.

Thus law comes from many sources, and these sources are all connected in the web of government. The lawyer's task is one requiring patience in searching out these sources. For the law is not a simple book of rules found in one place. It is the accumulated growth of the wisdom and experience of men working in many places and observing man's activity from many sides.

8

THE ADVERSARY SYSTEM

Pathways to Truth

Some ancient Chinese philosopher must have remarked that there are many roads by which men go to seek the truth and who can say which is the shortest.

The way in which the truth is sought in the legal system is one of the most interesting aspects of the profession and one of the least understood by laymen. Thus, before we begin a discussion of cases and of thinking like a lawyer, we ought to examine the legal institution known as the trial.

When the chemist is confronted by an unknown substance, the nature of which he wishes to establish, he takes it with him into his laboratory and there subjects it to all known tests. When he has discovered the nature of the unknown substance, he publishes his findings as part of man's knowledge about the universe. When lawyers are in dispute as to the validity of a proposition and it is necessary that it be settled, they resort to the legal institution of the trial before a court. When the procedures of the trial have been complied with, the court deliberates and decides the matter in dispute. This decision then becomes part of man's knowledge about the law. Neither the chemist nor the judge claims for his finding that it represents ultimate truth, but each asserts it as a valid proposition in the light of his method of seeking for truth.

The institution of the trial is one of the ancient cornerstones of the legal system.   History is filled with famous examples: Solomon deciding which of the two mothers rightfully claimed the living child, the trial of Jesus before Pilate, the trial of Jeanne d'Arc.   The forms by which the trial is conducted have changed with the centuries, but the essential idea of appeal to higher authority has remained constant.   In your history you will read of earlier forms of trial, such as the trial by ordeal, in which the party who asserted the truth of his statement seized a hot iron in his bare hands and if the wound healed within a certain number of days, that was proof of the validity of his claim.   Fortunately, we no longer rely upon this method.

The Trial and Man's Rights

Around the institution of the trial are centered some of our most cherished liberties, for which men have fought and died. Among these is the right of each person to have access to the courts for the trial of his disputes.   We have come to take this right so much for granted that we are inclined to forget that it has not always been ours.   Among these also is our concept that each person, strong or weak, rich or poor, is equal in his standing before the court of law.   We hear charges of violation of this concept, and, if true, these are to be deplored, but we must also be aware of that which we do not hear, because it is not "news," namely, the many, many instances in which this right is scrupulously observed.   In order to preserve these rights, we have placed around them many protections.   The man who is too poor to pay the costs of his law suit is permitted to take an oath to that effect and bring suit *in forma pauperis,* the costs being borne by the government.   The man who has reason to believe that the court before which his case is to be heard is prejudiced against him personally has the privilege of having an unbiassed tribunal hear his case.   The man who cannot afford to employ an attorney to aid him in the protection of his asserted rights is now, in most jurisdictions, assured of advice of counsel through legal aid clinics and lawyer-reference plans sponsored by the local bar associations.

We have already referred to the right of trial by jury, considered so important that it was embodied in the constitution. The great writ of *habeas corpus,* by which a court may order that a man be produced before it to learn the nature of the crime with which he has been charged, lest he languish unheeded in jail, is one of the great bulwarks against tyranny. These are but a few of the great rights and liberties which have grown up with their central focus upon the concept of a trial. You will come to be familiar with many others as you proceed with your study of law.

The Nature of Our Trial System

We are now ready to look at certain features of the trial itself. The trial is thought of as an appeal to higher authority for decision of a legal dispute. For example, two men, disputing a claim, may either fight out the matter or take it to a higher authority to decide. Since fighting may well constitute a violation of the criminal law, leading to unpleasant consequences, men are encouraged to resort to the alternative measures provided by society for settling disputes. A glance at the present position of international law may serve to illustrate. Nations, disputing claims, have resorted to war to effect a solution. International law, as represented in such institutions as the United Nations, is seeking to persuade nations to abandon resort to war and to accept the alternative measures provided by arbitration, resort to the International Court of Justice, and similar peaceful methods. The concept of the trial by law is an alternative to that of the trial by force.

By resort to higher authority in our legal system we mean

going to the courts. However, as we said earlier, it does not mean going to just any court: it means going to a court which has jurisdiction (authority) to hear and decide the dispute.

This court then proceeds to hear and decide the legal dispute submitted to it. Courts in our legal system do not ordinarily give advisory opinions. They decide disputes or controversies in which the disputing parties represent interests which are adverse to one another and ripe for decision. This is what we mean by the adversary system, which is characteristic of our trials. The theory is that the parties, being adverse and in dispute, will develop fully before the court all the disputed points upon which the court is expected to give a decision. The court is to see that each party has "his day in court," that "fair play" or "due process" is given each party, that only proper evidence is presented, that the authorized procedure is followed in presenting the dispute, and that no prejudicial acts are committed by either side before the court.

Within these prescribed limits and under these rules, the parties are to dispute out the matter, presenting their evidence and testimony and refuting or explaining away that presented by the other side. Then the dispute between the parties, having been fully explored and aired, is presented to the court to decide. It is important to remember that the court decides that dispute as it was presented to it and not the dispute as it might have been presented had the parties been better prepared or abler in argument.

This is the adversary system in theory as well as to a large extent in practice. However, it is only fair to state that modern judges do at times inject themselves into the trial, sometimes by questioning the witnesses themselves or by giving counsel an opportunity to amend their position, where to do otherwise would be to do injustice to the client, and by doing independent research into the points of law involved.

Faults and Merits of the Adversary System

The adversary nature of the proceedings and the fact that responsibility is placed squarely upon the parties to present their case fully make the trial assume, as one writer has pointed out, some of the aspects of a tournament, in which the parties contend before a judge as referee. You will also hear arguments made that this system gives undue advantage to the party who can retain the best lawyer. The layman, who sees the lawyers going at one another hammer and tongs in the courtroom, only to engage in friendly conversation later in the corridor, is quite apt to consider lawyers as an insincere lot. Still others will say to you that lawyers are so fond of arguments and fees that they do not care which side of a case they represent.

Some of these questions may be in your mind as you decide whether to study law. Most lawyers at one time or another have weighed them and made decisions themselves. There is no easy answer. But there are a few things which it is well to keep in mind. In our society, we believe that the important thing is that every person aggrieved should have a chance to present that legal grievance to a court in as full and fair a fashion as possible. To that end lawyers are trained: they serve to see that men are aided in presenting their cases. In the decision of nearly every case, there is a winning and a losing side. This does not mean that every lawyer who loses a case should not have brought it; nor does it mean that every lawyer who defends a man charged with the commission of a crime and loses was morally at fault in defending the man. It is a cardinal principle of our law that every man shall be presumed to be innocent until he is proved guilty. Further, in our society we have placed the responsibility for decision on the court.   It is true that the court relies upon the aid and advice of the lawyers before it, but it alone decides.   So great is this responsibility that our society has provided that in cases where the court is believed to have been in error, its decision may be reviewed by a series of appellate courts.

The adversary system may not in all cases produce a result which all men agree upon as just.   However, in the course of its history, many changes have been made in its procedure to assure that it be made as perfect as possible.   In a fallible world, it is as good as man has yet been able to devise and agree upon.

9

THE STUBBORN FACTS

The Case-book

The form in which you will first meet the sources of law in the classroom will be the so-called "case-book." This is a compilation of selected cases, statutes, rulings of administrative agencies, law review and textbook excerpts, and portions of the Restatements of the Law. These materials, plus the discussion by your instructor either in answer to specific questions or in exploring further a point of law, will form the standard substance from which you will set out to learn about law.

There are several things which should be said about the case-book. It represents a teaching-learning instrument. It does not purport to contain all the cases on a given subject. Neither does it set itself up as the only instrument from which law can be learned. It is a selection of materials chosen by the author for teaching purposes. The criteria used by authors in selecting the cases vary. Some authors maintain that the good case-book should be a "parade of horribles," cases which can readily be criticised by students because they proceed on unsound assumptions, and statutes which somehow fail to meet the problems at hand. The notion here is that such cases and such statutes provide the maximum opportunity for class discussion and criticism. Others maintain that a good case-book should contain only the great landmark cases. In this way, the author believes, the student will learn "sound" law and come in contact with the great judges and the dominant ideas. Still others maintain and act upon the assumption that the most recent cases are the best ones, because they permit the student and instructor to evaluate the decision against the background of their own current experience. There are many variations on these themes, and the definitive version of the case-book has not yet been written. In passing, it should be mentioned that the case-book is a distinctly American instructional idea, originating at Harvard under Langdell and copied with various changes in all national law schools.

One of the acknowledged deficiencies of the case-book as a sole instrument for law study is the fact that, being a compilation of cases, it introduces you only to those problems or disputes which were actually litigated before courts, and not to those which were ironed out in consultation or arbitration in the lawyer's office or to those relationships which passed off amicably as the parties had intended without dispute or the necessity of reference to a court. Certainly it is true that only a very small percentage of the total number of contracts made ever result in litigation. The sound lawyer draws his contracts for a client so as to render litigation unnecessary rather than to invite it. Though the fact is recognized that case-book study is primarily litigation study, it is difficult to present non-litigation materials, since official reports of such are difficult to find. Hence in the classroom your instructor will help you to draw out of the litigated case reports the experience necessary for your learning how to avoid the legal difficulty of which the case is an illustration.

It is also true that case-books in the main concentrate on presenting reports of cases which have been appealed to higher courts and hence you learn primarily about the cases in the highest courts rather than about cases in courts of first instance or trial courts. Occasionally you will find case-books which contain reports of actual trials. The reason why more are not included is a practical one. Trial cases, except in the federal courts, are rarely printed officially and hence are usually unavailable to editors of case-books in official form. Further, the reports of actual trials are so lengthy that only a few of them could be included in a case-book of normal size, which would greatly limit the book's usefulness.

You will also notice that these case-books contain cases from many jurisdictions and not simply from the one in which you plan to practice. Side by side in the book you may find the law as announced by the highest courts in California and Australia. This experience will aid you in appreciating the meaning of the phrase "common law" as a body of ideas worthy of consideration wherever the Anglo-American system prevails. You are being prepared in the common legal ideas which form our joint heritage.

How to Use the Case-book

Now with regard to your use of the case-book, it cannot be overemphasized, although it frequently falls on deaf ears, that the best avenue to reading such a book is to examine first the preface and table of contents. In the preface, the author usually reveals his "slant" or point of view in writing or compiling the case-book, as well as his ideas as to what this particular course is all about. The table of contents presents you with a sort of ready-made outline for the course, arranged in topics and sub-topics. Here is the framework upon which the selected cases and materials are hung. You can assume that the cases contained in a certain section or sub-section have

been placed there by the author because they serve to illustrate or to develop the main heading of that section.   It is
amazing how much help this can be to you in learning the law
of a course when you come upon those cases which seem to
defy classification.   Unless the author of the book is a sadist,
each case was put there for a specific purpose of furthering
his outline, and often your instructor will ask you, "Why
did the author include this case?" or "How does this case
further our knowledge of this particular subject?"   Of
course, you must not be surprised if the instructor says, "We
will skip the next case, since it seems to add nothing but confusion."   You will soon discover that almost every instructor
secretly considers that the only really good case-book would
be one which he has compiled himself.

There are certain things which you are expected to do with
this case-book, the first of which is to read the assigned cases.
This does not mean reading after the manner of a novel, skim-
ming lightly for the thread of plot.   It means reading them
as carefully as you would a page of mathematics or chemistry
or biology.   You should read each word, looking up the
unknown words in a legal dictionary, which at this stage ought
to be at your elbow.   The old proverb "To read many times
is not necessarily to understand" is worth cherishing, plain
as it is.   Sometimes the case-book editor delights in choosing a first case which contains a healthy supply of Latin and
even Norman French terms.   This is not done solely to annoy
and baffle you (as it usually does) or to deter you from studying law as a profession, nor is it done by the author to show
off his erudition.   It is intended to send you to a legal dictionary or a senior law student, and since frequently the
whole point of the case is found or made intelligible only
through the Latin tag, it instructs you in the necessity of
reading each word intelligently.

Other case-book editors may include as a first case one which turns on an ancient procedural device, frequently one no longer used and to be discovered only in a dictionary. Again this serves not only as a sign-post to the dictionary, but also as a method of instructing you in the mysteries of procedure by illustrating the important rôle which the existence of a remedy plays in the law. Sometimes you will discover that the first case is included to serve as a springboard for the instructor to develop the historical background of the course.

Briefing or Abstracting Cases

Having read this case, you will be expected to prepare what is variously called an abstract, or brief, or *précis* of the case. This is a digested version of the case. Almost every instructor has his own particular picture of what a well-formed brief or abstract will be. Sometimes, he will instruct you in briefing cases in an introductory lecture. More frequently, you will learn what he expects by his criticisms of your own products in class. Do not be surprised if that which one instructor considers to be a good brief will be rejected by another as insufficient or too long. Perhaps it is not too wide of the mark to say that the best brief for any instructor is the one he has previously made for himself.

Even so, let us approach the problem of briefing by an examination of the functions which it is to perform for you. If a brief or abstract performs these functions, then it is a useful one. The brief is to remind you in class of the salient facts and points of law raised and decided in the case. One of the time-worn requests of first year instructors is to ask you to "state" a given case, and it is here that a well drawn abstract will help to refresh your memory. If the brief be too long, you will lose the salient points in the verbiage.   There is a tendency among first-year students to make their briefs too long, largely because at that stage everything seems strange and important to them.   It is interesting to note how your briefs will shrink in size as you become more adept at spotting important points.   <u>A further function of the brief is as an aid in reviewing the course for examinations</u>.   Instead of an attempt to accomplish the impossible task of rereading all the cases, reference to the briefs should serve to recall the problems to mind.   Hence the brief should have enough details to recall for you the problems and the pertinent approaches advanced in class discussion.

<u>The most important function performed by briefing or abstracting cases is that of giving you training in analysis</u>.   You are to read an appellate court opinion, which is normally already the product of careful condensation, and are asked to dehydrate that report still further without losing any of its essential flavor.   It is such a task as the editors of *Reader's Digest* must do.

If you are to eliminate from the report what is nonessential, it is necessary for you first to decide what is essential.   One of the keen tasks of being a lawyer is this kind of selection. The briefing of cases is your first plunge into training in this field.   It is for this reason that law school instructors insist that you prepare your own briefs.   He knows that so-called "canned briefs" can be purchased generally, prepared to fit any case-book, but he also knows that for training in analysis they are both useless and harmful.   They provide the information, but someone else has had the benefit.   The prospective surgeon who would get someone else to do his anatomy "labs" is no more dangerous than the lawyer who has shirked the basic training in analysis.

For the same reason, the use of briefs prepared by someone else (a colleague or last year's honor student) will not instruct you in analysis, although it may go undetected in class and save you time. Only by getting down and digging the abstracts out yourself can you perform this function. You will probably dislike briefing cases, in much the same way that you may have disliked working out calculus problems, but it is a necessary chore. Many say that what you will carry away from law school is not so much the specific rules of law in the cases in the case-book, but the knowledge of how to get the law out of the cases.

Finding the Facts

Getting at the law of a case involves the whole task of analysis, and it is with this task that we must now deal in detail. We will break it down into three aspects: the facts, the problems, and the law rules. In this chapter, we will deal with the facts.

Earlier we said that cases deal with people and with events which affect their lives. The trial and judgment of a case are themselves facts in history. When you read the report of a case, you are coming in at the final stage of a long process. It is as if you were reading the review of a play you had not seen. The case report usually begins with a statement of the facts. This is the final distilled version of the most salient facts in the opinion of the court. It represents perhaps volumes of testimony, exhibits, and pleadings which the counsel have filed with the court, plus their arguments and briefs. Even were we to get all of these papers and pull the facts out of them, we still would know nothing of the conferences between lawyers and clients, the memoranda written, the investigations made in that case.

If by chance we possessed all of these, then we might be said to have available all of the known facts about this dispute. If then we observed which of the mass of facts the attorney chose as material, we might be able to learn from all this the method of analysis used by the legal mind. Even so, we would be working from the finished end of the product rather than from the beginning, and it is the beginning in which we are now interested.

Therefore, let us attempt to go back to the beginning of the drama. It is a task in which the case-book will help only incidentally, and it is one of the most neglected areas of law study. Let us go back to the time when the client came into the lawyer's office with the problem which ultimately became the subject of the case in the book. The client came in about a series of transactions which occurred, say, nine months ago. Obviously, the first step is to find out what the client's problem is all about, namely, to discover the facts. At this stage the client is the source of the facts. He tells his story of the events of nine months ago as he recalls them. The lawyer urges him to tell all that he can remember and to produce such documents as he possesses which bear on these transactions. This stage is analogous to the case history which the doctor takes from his patient prior to examination.

The lawyer, like the doctor, soon comes to ask certain routine questions, which he has learned to ask because of his past experience and training in such matters. It is well to realize that this stage is not easy. The client may omit facts innocently or intentionally, either because he considers them to be of no importance or because they do not reflect creditably upon his claim. The client may be confused about his recollections. It is the first job of the lawyer to pull forth patiently but firmly all of his client's recollections about this transaction, whether or not they are contradictory and whether or not they may in the end prove satisfactory or important.

Having learned all that he can from his client, the lawyer sets out to learn all that can be known about that series of transactions involved in his client's story. At this stage, the lawyer is like the historian. He tracks to ground all relevant documents. He interviews as many people as he has reason to believe have information and will give it to him. He reads all that he can find on the subject. He is also like the detective. He tries to piece together each bit of information until the jigsaw puzzle is complete. Always there are gaps, and always the gaps contain the challenge. Always there are stubborn facts which cannot be fitted into the picture or which elude even the most careful search.

The result should be that the lawyer knows more about those particular transactions than even the client himself; certainly as much as, and preferably more than, the counsel for the other side. Now that he is possessed of all the available facts (we soon learn that we can never have them all) and has put them in some order, noting the contradictions and weak links, he turns to the next process, which distinguishes the legal method. Up to this point, he might have been acting as a historian, as a scientist, as a detective, or as a man gathering material for a novel or biography. Now he stands off and looks at the whole picture made by the assembled facts and begins to select from them those which have legal significance. If he were a doctor, he would seek facts having medical significance.

This, then, is the first step to be taken as you read the case in the case-book. What were the facts involved in the case? Which ones did the court consider to be the most important? Which ones did the court treat as irrelevant? Which ones could be said to constitute the turning point of the decision?

You may well ask, "If law schools do little in this particular skill of fact-finding and it is important to me, then how can I train myself in this skill?" Simply by setting exercises for yourself.   Set yourself the task of describing in minute detail your actions of last evening.   Having witnessed a certain accident, describe for yourself the events as you saw them.   Or describe your actions as a motorist driving to the university this morning and consider how you would set about proving them.   Check as to the evidence which you possess with regard to your admisison to law school. These are sufficient to suggest other exercises to you.   By making yourself answer these questions and do these exercises, you will learn how to ask questions of other people and also what difficulties may be encountered in answering them.   Thus you can train yourself to be observant and to ferret out the stubborn facts.

You may ask whether there are not certain short cuts which can be used in getting at the facts.   Must one always aim at getting all of them?   Of course these are short cuts. Some are legitimate; some are dangerous.   But just as you must ordinarily learn to walk before you learn to run, so the beginner must learn to do a thorough job, for his own protection as well as that of his clients.   After you have been doing this work for a long time, then you can try the short cuts, because you will then understand what you are short-cutting and the calculated risk involved.

Perhaps enough has been said to indicate the importance of this first step, the acquisition of a decent respect for the facts, particularly stubborn ones, plus the realization that no matter how hard you dig, you can never capture them all, and that hence you must concentrate on those which prior wisdom has deemed to have the greatest amount of legal significance.

10

THE LEGAL PROBLEM

You do not have to be very old or very wise to discover that the world is very full of problems. However simple it was when God created it, man has contrived to make it an exceedingly complex place. In fact, we find in our society that a considerable segment of the population is devoted to the business of problem-solving. The physician, lawyer, priest or minister, psychiatrist, and tax consultant are among this group of problem-solvers.

Lawyers, as problem-solvers, are interested only in those problems which are legal in nature. Before the lawyer can do much about solving the problem, it is axiomatic that he should know what the problem is. The world is unfortunately quite full of proposed solutions to problems which the solver has either not bothered to think through or has failed utterly to understand. We do not need more of such solutions. The doctor who has carefully analyzed his patient's condition and reached a sound diagnosis knows the problem with which he must grapple. The lawyer who has studied his client's case with all his skill and care knows where to seek for a solution. <u>The man, be he lawyer or doctor, who does not or cannot see the problem, shoots in the dark and wastes his fire—not to mention his client's time and money</u>.

It is no exaggeration to say that the great bulk of legal training is directed toward cultivating your ability to spot

legal problems and to know what to do about them.   It is a
truism that the man who can best detect and understand a
problem usually is the man who has had the most thorough
experience in the matter.   The log-man who built my moun-
tain cabin and instructed me in the art of log-building used
to say that it takes many years of looking at and handling
logs to be able to tell at a glance just how a log will lie in
a cabin wall.

Identifying the Problem

We can begin by saying that the best way to start is to learn
through experience just what legal problems look like.   Unlike the medical schools, where you can get experience from
work in the laboratories and hospitals, the law schools must
train their students by concentrating on the lessons of past
experience through a careful study of cases, statutes, and legal
writings.

The law student is trained to spot legal problems in much
the same way as a bird dog is trained.   First, he is introduced to already-spotted legal problems so that he can
note and learn their characteristics.   Every case which you
study in your case-book represents the result of lawyers'
and courts' addressing themselves to a legal problem, describing it, noting its characteristics, and commenting on its
boundaries.   Sometimes you will read in the court's opinion
the statement, "The complainant has not stated a cause of
action to the court."   This means that the party has not
presented to the court a problem containing those elements or
characteristics which the court regards as necessary to make
a "legal problem" upon which the court has power to act.
It may well constitute a personal problem or an economic
one worrisome to the complainant, but unless it is a legal one,
the court may well refuse to act.

Let us take an example: A strong swimmer who watches from the bank of a river the drowning of a man whom he could easily save may from a social or moral point of view be a cad and a scoundrel, but the relatives of the drowned man have no action against the swimmer for his lack of concern for the deceased. This is a moral problem but not a legal one. The suitor who promises marriage and then thinks better of it may cause the lady in question great anguish and embarrassment, and yet in many jurisdictions his actions causing her harm do not create a legal problem. Or again, the newspaper which for the purpose of reader-appeal or increased circulation reprints in detail the facts of notorious criminal trials may cause great humiliation and distress to innocent people who were connected with the trial and who have tried to forget it, but some courts have felt that such actions do not create a legal problem.

Thus, you will study the cases in the books in order to discover just what problems courts consider to be legal ones, which ones they have refused to admit as such, and what steps and reasoning they used to arrive at these conclusions. We learn from their experience. We see what they treat as essential and why they do so, and from this knowledge we can then chart and predict future action.

Learning from Past Problems

Further, we will learn that in the early period of Anglo-American law the existence of a legal problem was determined by whether the facts presented would fit into one of the available writs as prescribed by the king's court. If that which had happened to you corresponded to that which the king's writ described as a wrong, then your request for a remedy was legitimate. Thus it was often said that where there was a writ, there was a remedy, or conversely, no writ—

no remedy.   We might say that in this period legal problems were those described in writs and the lawyer who knew his writs by heart could spot his legal problems easily.   During this early period, the legal problems took the names of the writs, for example, trespass, nuisance, debt, and so on.

You will also discover as you proceed in your studies that new writs were formed to meet new situations; that old writs were by fiction or interpretation extended to cover new problems; that some writs became obsolete; that some writs became so all-embracing as to become almost meaningless forms; that finally the whole writ system was swept away and a single form of action substituted in most jurisdictions.   But the old learning and experience were not swept aside overnight: as Maitland remarked, "the forms of action are buried but they continue to rule us from their graves."   The old names clung: trespass, debt, indebitatus assumpsit, conversion, and so forth.   Judges continued to appraise allegedly new legal problems by measuring them against the old experience.   This is a long and complex story, involving as it does some of the most interesting pages of English and American history.   It is not to be expected that this cursory glance will do more than inform you that in many instances you can spot a legal problem by seeing whether it contains those characteristics formerly embodied in the old system of named actions.   If it does, then it is probably still a legal problem or, as some may call it, a "cause of action."

As you study your cases, you will also discover that some problems in earlier times would be "legal problems" in courts of law but not in courts of equity, and vice versa. Again, this stems from the fact that some problems had no remedies in the ordinary law courts but for these same problems the chancellor in equity would provide a remedy. Similarly, it was said that a court of equity would not give a remedy if one were available in a court of law. During a long period of Anglo-American legal history, there were separate courts and judges administering these remedies and it sometimes happened that if you got in the wrong court with your problem you were turned away. Ultimately, as you will learn, in most jurisdictions law and equity were joined and such remedies as either system had previously given were available in a single set of courts.

Thus, in your law school study one way in which you will learn to spot legal problems is by observing the experience of lawyers and courts in past cases. By looking at these we train ourselves to recognize a legal problem when we are faced by it in our own experience. In this respect we are like the child who, having seen elephants pictured in the alphabet book, suddenly sees one in a zoo and says, "Look, there is an elephant." But this is not the sole path of our search. It may have once been true to say that the common or case law was the rule and the statute the exception in the great sweep of the law canvas, yet so great has been the legislative activity of recent years that we find Mr. Justice Frankfurter writing that among the cases which have come recently to the Supreme Court of the United States less than one percent have involved common law and over ninety-nine percent have involved statutes. Even so, only a small percentage of the statutes passed result in litigation. Hence we turn to a study of the statutes themselves to discover the legal problems.

Clues in the Statutes

We study, for example, the statutes on the creation of corporations, on negotiable instruments, on insurance, on the issuance of securities, on patents and trade-marks, so that we may become cognizant of the legal problems which they take as their province.   Here we are frequently without court guidance as to the meaning of the terms of a statute.   We must turn to the rules and general principles laid down by courts and writers for the construction of statutes.   Some law schools have put into their curricula special courses in legislation, devoted largely to the problem of construing statutes. In general, we will find that what is sought is the intention of the legislature as expressed in its enacted words.   We will look at the problem with which the legislature said it was concerned.   In some instances, we will look at the reports of the legislative committees which held the hearings on the problem and drafted the legislation.   In other words, we will seek to find what the problem was that the legislature made into a legal problem by enacting legislation.   For example, just prior to the passing of the Interstate Commerce Act of 1887, the charges which railroads made for their service in interstate commerce presented no legal problem in federal law.   It was an economic matter, subject only to such interference as state laws provided.   After 1887, this became a federal legal problem, and railroads and their lawyers had to appraise the meaning and applicability of the statute to what had previously been a management problem.

In this statutory search we would include also the rulings and regulations and the decisions and opinions of administrative agencies.   For example, a discussion of the legal problems involved in taxation would be very incomplete if we did not include the rulings and regulations of the Commissioner of Internal Revenue.   Similarly, the orders of the Securities and Exchange Commission and its rules and regulations are indispensable to an understanding of the legal problems arising out of corporate finance.

Problems of Tomorrow

It is certainly true that there are far more legal problems than ever before. This has come about both through the greater complexity of life itself and also through the increased activities of government in all its branches and forms. There are those who point out that we seem to live in an age in which the panacea for ills is thought to be legislation. It is far safer for a lawyer today to guess that the problem before him is a legal one than it was in earlier times.

If, then, the law schools were to meet the task of training you to spot legal problems merely by putting you through the paces of already-spotted problems in decided cases and enacted statutes, they would not fulfil their function adequately. This prepares you only to spot problems in an age which is already past. The student is not to meet problems and to decide about them in 1760 or 1900 or even at the time of his law study. His days are yet to come, and in a changing world it is not likely that the categories of legal problems will remain unchanged.

Hence in your class discussion of cases and statutes, your instructor will reach into the future as best he can and anticipate new problems now in process of formation. He will do this by posing to you a wealth of hypothetical problems, slightly different from the cases in the book, encouraging you to reach out from known ground into new territory. He will pull out passages in the court's opinion, sometimes written as dicta, which seem to indicate the path new developments in the law are likely to take, and he will ask you to comment on these passages. Or he will refer you to legal writings in which the author speaks of the inadequacies of present remedies to meet problems and urges a course of action for the future. The greater the training in these hypothetical problems, the more flexible becomes your ability to ferret out potential legal problems. Here you will practice the useful devices of extension by analogy, *reductio ad absurdum,* and all the tools of the logician's kit, as well as the findings and statistics of the scientist and the fact-gatherer.

It is frequently said that the law school examinations represent excursions into a sort of Dali landscape, far-fetched and grim from the view of ordinary life. But there is method in your instructor's apparent madness. By means of these bizarre and contorted fact-situations, he presents to you the opportunity to apply your problem-finding techniques.

This, then, is the course of training: from the old problems in the decided cases, through the borderline problems as evidenced by conflicting decisions, then to the statutes where you must dig for the problem even before the court speaks, and finally on to the emerging future problems. As we said at the outset, the man who can see the problem has part of his battle finished, because he then knows what it is with which he must grapple. The isolation of the cause of poliomyelitis will be the important beginning of the attack upon the disease. Again, we must stress the need for exactness in defining the problem. A faulty diagnosis or an incomplete one not only wastes the doctor's and the patient's time, but may prove harmful to both. The same is true of the lawyer and his client. The man who looks carelessly will see carelessly. It requires patience and skill to look and look again until that which you see bears the closest possible resemblance to that which is.

The whole preoccupation with the search for the facts about which we spoke in the previous chapter was in order that we might discover the legal problem. The more we search out the facts, the less apt we are to accept too-easy and over-generalized labels. The more one learns about his problem, the more certain he is that it is unique, being more or less like this one or that one, possessing some of the qualities of each, but possessed also of some small part of difference. The lawyer and the physician both have come to speak a careful, much qualified language, exasperating to outsiders, important to those on the inside. Neither, in his field, is a dogmatist. The words "perhaps" or "not exactly" become part and parcel of their daily talk.

11

THE LAW RULES

We have now explored two aspects of the method of thinking like a lawyer. First, we saw that it was advisable to gather all the facts about a situation before us and then attempt to sort out these facts into categories: those which have legal significance, those which have none, and those which may or may not be of legal import depending on the course of action taken. To take a simple illustration: Jim comes into your office and states that his motor car has been taken from him without his permission and not returned; that he believes that John, red haired and with an invalid wife, took the car to get some medicine for his wife. Assuming that all these statements can be proved, we will probably decide that the facts of legal significance are that Jim was in possession of the car and that John took it without consent or right. We will also decide that the color of John's hair and the health of his wife are of no legal significance in this matter. John's motive in taking the car will also be of no legal significance.

Second, we saw that we should examine the whole factual picture in order to determine whether as a whole it presents one or more legal problems or no legal problem at all. This finding of a legal problem usually leads to a tentative diagnosis of the matter.

The Lawyer Distinguished from the Physician

We are now ready to turn to look at the tools which are available to lawyers in attacking problems. These we shall call the "law rules." Here we depart from the analogy to the medical profession which we have been following. The physician, having reached a tentative diagnosis of his patient's illness, begins to take measures himself in the light of his diagnosis. He is the arbiter of the methods to be used in the patient's behalf, and the proof of the remedy lies in the recovery of the patient. All the accumulated written wisdom of great practitioners, all the laboratory technical services, all the products of pharmaceutical development are available to him, but once the patient has placed himself in the physician's hands for action, it is the physician who decides what should be done.

The lawyer, on the other hand, knows that however satisfying his diagnosis and advised action may be to him or to his client, yet the ultimate word as to the remedy for the legal problem lies not with him but with a third factor, not lawyer, not client—namely, the court. Hence, not only must the tenative diagnosis appear to be sound to the lawyer and his client, but it must also have a fair chance of being accepted as sound within the framework of the law rules as seen by a court.

It is true that there are many instances in which the lawyer performs services for his client without any court intervention, but even when a client is pleased by a contract drawn by his lawyer, the lawyer is aware that if the contract is challenged or not performed, then a court will pass upon the appropriateness and validity of his action. This distinction between the functions of the lawyer and the physician is a profound one. If physicians, before attempting action, had to plead before a board of the medical association, which had power to grant or withhold the remedy, they would understand a bit better the lawyer's delays and the seeming uncertainty of the lawyer's position.

Kinds of Law Rules

The law rules comprise the accumulated pronouncements of those agencies in society which possess authority to prescribe legal standards and rules of behavior. As we have seen earlier, these agencies include courts, legislatures, executives, and administrative agencies.

These law rules include what we call rules of substantive law, for example, the legal requirements for making a valid contract or will or deed, the designation of rights in land, the forms by which a valid marriage is contracted. They also include the rules of adjective law, for example, the rules by which rights are enforced and remedies are requested.

Some of these law rules consist of detailed requirements, for example, the motor vehicle rules of the road prescribing the distance at which one car shall follow another, the signals for indicating turns, or the number of lights to be displayed by vehicles. Other law rules are in the form of general standards, such as the maxim in the law of nuisance which provides that every man shall so use his own property as not to damage his neighbor, or the concept that obligations are to be performed in good faith.

Some of the law rules are peculiar to one state or jurisdiction; for example, the laws concerning community property of husband and wife prevail in some states and not in others. Some actions constitute crimes in one state but not in another. Others of the law rules are found to exist in almost identical form in all jurisdictions, for example, the negotiable instruments law.

Fallacies About the Law Rules

The law rules are the stock in trade of the lawyer, and hence they are the meat of the law student's study. There are certain fallacies prevalent among laymen and beginning law students which should be dealt with early in our discussion. One of these is that there exists somewhere a book, probably bound in black, containing all the law rules, neatly indexed and arranged, like the answer section which used to appear in the back of arithmetic books. Not even the most optimistic advertising "blurb" of the law book publishers can seriously make this claim; neither can the most ardent supporters of the system of codified law dogmatically assert it. Even the Emperors Justinian and Napoleon, despite their monumental efforts at codification of all law and their hopes that such would be the exclusive and permanent law collection, saw their hopes dashed

There are and have been many attempts to collect the laws into one set of volumes, but at best these compilers can only offer secondary sources which must frequently be modified and brought up to date. There are also to be found extremely helpful loose-leaf services which keep you abreast of the many changes in the legal rules affecting a particular topic, but these too are only guides to the law, and are not the whole law itself.

The law rules, for the most part, still have to be dug out of many scattered places, painstakingly and with the consuming of much midnight oil. As we have seen, the case-books, from which you will study the law rules, contain only an exceedingly small fragment of the applicable law. As students, you may perhaps feel that your instructor possesses a book in which all the law is set out, which he could pass on to you if he would, but which in his perverseness he keeps to himself. There is no such book. The client may feel that his lawyer has only to reach into the drawer of his desk to answer his question and that he ponders and searches only to make his fee seem reasonable. The man who can find such a book will possess a treasure as valuable as a formula for curing baldness.

The second fallacy is the too-widely held notion that the law rules are certain, immutable, and unambiguous. The law student soon learns that the world can still go on and men appear rational although the highest court in Illinois may reach a decision exactly contrary to that of Massachusetts on what appear to be identical facts, and although both of these courts may differ from their sister court in California. Frequently courts of equal rank within the same state differ as to what the law is in that state. As long as reasonable men may differ reasonably, such will be the case.

The law student also learns that reasonable men and reasonable judges may differ widely as to the meaning of a word in a statute; that the same court has on occasion reversed itself. The course in constitutional law will afford many examples of this phenomenon. There are, it is true, many areas of the law where agreement among the courts is general and has been so for a considerable period of time. We like to think of law as being permanent and unchanging, and yet we are perfectly aware of the fact that law follows and works upon life, which we know to be in a state of flux. Perhaps it has always been said, but of recent years it has been said more frequently by many learned commentators that "law is what the courts say it is" or "law is what is enforced" or "law depends on, among other things, what the particular judge had for breakfast or the temperament of the judge's wife." These writers have rediscovered the fact that law is a human institution, written in man's language, and applied and interpreted by human beings called judges. This has always been so. In their criticism of the old notion that laws, not men, governed, they have overstressed the contrary notion that men, having made laws, mold them and their words to changing needs and desires.

Security of Transactions versus Growth of Law

Law, as we will come to know it in law study, is perhaps more resistant to change than other comparable human institutions. In your courses in sociology and in economics you will hear much about the charge that laws lag far behind the advances in knowledge of the social sciences. Lawyers and lawmakers are traditionally supposed to be more cautious than other folk. Then, too, in the main, most of us want the law to be certain and unchanging because we wish to feel that in the realm of law the future is somewhat predictable. This we sometimes call the "security of transactions." The man who makes a contract today wishes to know that the laws governing that contract will continue in force at least for the life of the contract. The man who makes a will disposing of his property wishes the security of knowing that the will is to be honored on his death. The man or woman who is married according to the legal forms prescribed for marriage wishes assurance that he or she will not find the marriage annulled by later legislation. These and many other reasons make for the desire that the law be stable and predictable.

Operating in the same arena with this idea of the security of transactions is the concern which men feel that laws should develop in such a way as to produce greater approximations to justice and that where there is error it should be reformed. There have been great periods of reform in the history of law, either through legislation, as we have seen in the thirties, or through bold judicial action. We seem to be in an age

of transition when some of the old instances of the security of
transactions are being challenged by the appeal to "social
justice." As a law student you will soon learn that not all
the great legal controversies have been settled, that there is
still the challenge of new frontiers and new ideas, and that
you will be expected to provide responses to these challenges.
You will also find that men have provided different and conflicting laws and solutions for these problems. For example,
you will find that in the matter of divorce, Nevada has adopted
a far more lenient answer than most other states. You will
find that in some states a jilted wife or fiancée may sue one
who alienates the affections of her husband or suitor, while
in other states such actions, although once allowed, are now
outlawed by statute, and that in at least one jurisdiction a
judge has considered that the spouse has not lost anything but
"has merely learned something." Variety, while not providing certainty, has provided life and growth to the law.

When we turn to a specific consideration of the law rules,
we are entering upon the special realm of the lawyer. Up
to this point, when we spoke of the collection of the facts
or the ascertainment of a problem, we were as much in the
realm of the historian, economist, scientist, or logician as in
that of the lawyer. The methods used were to a large extent
the same. Although, for purposes of discussion, we have
divided the law-thinking process into chapters on facts, problems, rules, and hypotheses, yet in practice these stages are
closely interwoven. For example, the law rules determine
for us which of the facts possess legal significance. The law
rules also determine whether our facts as found constitute a
legal problem as presently recognized by our courts and
legislatures. The law rules will determine for us whether a
remedy is available for our problem and, lastly, the law rules
will determine the procedure by which we are to set forth our

legal problem to the proper court and show cause for the granting of that remedy.

Finding Law Rules in Cases

The discovery of the law rules is our prime task. Again, the law school approaches this task through the use of the case-book or through the recent variation of that instrument called "Cases and Materials," by which is meant that it includes not only cases but excerpts from statutes, law review and other doctrinal writings, reports, and forms. Already we have seen the case as a vehicle from which we can learn to approach facts and problems. It is also a means for getting at the law rules as announced and applied by the courts.

The traditional and perhaps simplest form of a law rule is the statement of some such proposition as this: If *A*, without consent or right, takes from the possession of *B* a thing of value and refuse to return it, then damages may be awarded to *B* for this loss. A less simple form may be: Where *A* undertakes gratuitously to perform a service for *B*, he is bound to perform it with due care. Our task with each case is to attempt to extract from the case the rules of law for which it may be said to be authority.

The case as reported will contain several things: the names of the parties, the court in which the case was tried, the date of the decision, a résumé of the pleadings and material facts, the decision or judgment of the court on the action before it, and the opinion of the court. Courts are expected to render opinions in support of their judgments. This is their report of their stewardship of the judicial power entrusted to them. Frequently, we may find not a single opinion but several opinions, some dissenting from the majority opinion, some concurring in the result but for different reasons.

From a study of these opinions, we seek to find the law

rules. What were the material facts which the court considered necessary to its decision?   Which of these facts did
the court consider to have been proved?   What was the
specific legal problem or issue raised by these facts?   What
was the required or proper disposition of the case?   Where
there is but one opinion and the judge has done this analysis
for you, your work is easy.   But where there are several
opinions, differing in reasoning but similar in final result, or
where there is a single opinion and it does not reveal the
framework of thought of the court, your task is difficult.
Here you must decide for yourself which of the statements
of the court are necessary to the decision of the case before
it and which are gratuitous remarks or dicta in that they
are not necessary to the decision of the case over which the
court had jurisdiction.   You will be guided by your instructor in this search for essentials, this sifting out from court
opinions of the specific propositions or rules of law set forth
in the case.

The simplest thing which we learn from our study of a
case is that if these exact facts were to occur again in that
jurisdiction, it is predictable that the same legal problem
would arise and that the rule or judgment previously given
would follow.   Some would argue that even this would not
be necessarily true unless all the other factors were the same,
including judges, lawyers, parties, and surrounding circumstances.   Too rigid a following of the argument would render
prediction impossible.   The lawyer and the law student are
interested in this element of predictability because it affords
a means whereby they can advise clients as to the possible
chances of success of their actions.   Sound predicability rests
of course on the concept that decisions previously reached by
courts on the basis of law rules announced will continue to
be honored by that court as binding.   This is usually referred

to as the doctrine of precedent and the result of the operation of the doctrine as *stare decisis*.   Little would be served at this time by entering into the timeworn discussion about "binding precedent" and *stare decisis*.   There is no gainsaying the truth that experience of the past lays a heavy and restraining hand upon the present and points a finger toward the future.   Whether we refer to it as "shackles" or as "received usages and wisdom" largely depends upon the context in which we are speaking.

Thus, though our first task is to learn precisely what has been decided in the past by courts and for what reasons, we wish also to investigate the extension of these rules to new situations.   To put the matter into symbols for a moment: where facts *A*, *B*, and *C* occur together, legal issue *Q* arises, upon which the *M* Supreme Court in 1938 has given judgment *Y*.   This constitutes the fact in history and, as we have said, upon this fact we build predictions reaching from the known into the unknown.   These take many forms, of which the following are but samples.   Where facts *A*, *B*, and *C* occur together, will the *O* Supreme Court consider that legal issue *Q* has arisen and render judgment *Y*?   Since each supreme court is supreme in its own realm, it is not bound by the decisions of courts in other states.   In theory, at least, we could have forty-eight different decisions on the same fact-situation, assuming so many variations possible.   In practice, courts do give ear to the experience of courts in other states, not as binding rules, but as persuasive and relevant indications of the way in which wisdom lies.   Hence, in law school you will study the decisions of many courts other than those in your own jurisdiction, on the assumption that sound reasoning knows no state boundaries.

Or again, where facts *A*, *B* and *C* occur but fact *B* occurs before facts *A* and *C*, will the Supreme Court of *M* consider that legal issue Q has arisen and render judgment Y?   Here we have the same court which rendered the judgment reported earlier, but now faced by the same facts in different sequence.   We must search the court's opinion to see whether the court in the earlier opinion considered the sequence of events to be important.   Here we may turn to the dicta in the case, where perhaps the judge stated that had the facts occurred in different sequence, issue R would have been presented and judgment S would have followed.   Thus we work with the decision which has been rendered and probe into the reasons which prompted it, in order to predict future action in a different case.   It sometimes happens that the dissenting opinion in one case later becomes the majority opinion in a later case, or again a strong dissent by a strong judge may well carry more weight persuasively than a contrary opinion by a less vigorous majority.   As you go through your cases, it will be interesting to note how many dissenting opinions by such men as Justices Brandeis and Holmes later came to be the majority view of the court on which they sat.

As we said before, these are but a few examples of the ways in which you can use the law rules as extracted from cases.   You will become very familiar with your instructor's questions "How would you apply the rules of this case to these facts?" or "How would you distinguish these decisions from your hypothetical case?" or "Are there any grounds upon which these contrary decisions can be reconciled?"   Little by little you come to appreciate these rules as useful implements with which to attack new and old problems.   To the lawyer, there is as much pleasure and satisfaction in a carefully drawn distinction or analogy as a physician must feel in a successful cure for a disease.

You will sometimes hear a case referred to as "on all fours" with another case. This means the case cannot be distinguished from an earlier one. As the lawyer grows in experience, he learns that actually no two cases are ever exactly alike, but sometimes the differences are not worth litigating. You may also hear lawyers say that they have just got a case for which they have been waiting, meaning that here is a case that presents the facts which will test and perhaps modify or overturn an old rule. Sometimes you will find a court which, while admitting that its decision based on earlier decisions does not provide a satisfactory solution to the problem, states that it is up to the legislature to provide a new rule by legislation. Occasionally, you will find a court which, while admitting that all the old law rules would point to a decision contrary to the one it renders, yet reasons from experience to a new conclusion and hence a new law rule.

Statutes

But, as we have pointed out earlier, cases are not the only sources of the law rules. Statutes in ever increasing numbers lay down law rules, and accordingly law schools must spend more time with the statutes.

Statutes themselves do many things. Some are special acts pertaining to one specific matter, such as the compensation of a named individual for damage caused to him by the state, or in earlier times the incorporation of railroads, canals, and turnpikes. The majority, however, are acts of general application. Some of these have as their purpose definition or delineation or delimitation, as for example those statutes which define the jurisdiction of certain courts or local government agencies, or those defining crimes or remedies. Others are enabling statutes granting rights or privileges—*e.g.*, those granting rights to third party beneficiaries under contracts, or setting forth the method of making a valid will or deed, or granting the franchise to women. Others serve to regulate conduct, such as statutes regulating the issuance of securities, safety practices on common carriers, the labelling of food and drugs, the construction of buildings in zoned areas, the preparation and serving of food in public places, the transportation of explosives, the flight of aircraft, the broadcasting of political addresses, and many other matters. Still other statutes have as their purpose the prohibition of certain acts, as for example the whole law of crimes, whether it be the commission of murder or the monopolizing of trade or commerce.

In the study of these statutes we are concerned with understanding exactly what the legislative rule means. What law rule did the legislature lay down? The problem is not whether the legislature was wise in doing what it did (although we will undoubtedly discuss this) but rather what the legislature actually did. Although many schools do not have courses in statutory law or legislation as such, yet in every law school such courses as procedure, corporations, trade regulation, negotiable instruments, sales, taxation, and administrative and constitutional law necessarily involve the handling of statutory materials. Courts have by no means done for us the whole job of interpreting the meaning of statutes. In the main they have only been called upon to interpret the most controversial passages.

The appreciation of exact meaning is an area of education we have only begun to explore, whether it be the meaning of legal symbols or of scientific or cultural ones. The continental law schools, which use enacted codes as their materials for study, have much to teach our common-law schools in the matter of the interpretation of statutes. Our schools have, however, made a fair beginning in the business. In an earlier chapter, we referred to the so-called canons or rules of statutory interpretation. Perhaps it is in order now to add slightly to those earlier remarks.

We begin with what we call the "plain meaning" rule. Where the meaning of a statute is clear and unambiguous on its face, then we are not entitled to go behind the statute to discover its meaning. For example, where an incorporation statute provides that there must be three natural persons of full age to serve as incorporators, the meaning of these words is plain and we have no doubt as to what must be done in order to comply with this section of the statute. We must of course admit that what may be clear to one person may be the opposite to another and hence in the last analysis it is the court which determines whether the language is plain, by passing upon it in a controverted case.

Where, however, the statute on its face is ambiguous as to its meaning, then either a court must clear up the ambiguity or else we must tackle the problem of meaning by ourselves. In many instances the legislative power intentionally uses terms of general meaning content, such as "good faith," "reasonable," "fair return," or "unfair methods of competition." In a few instances this has been held to be bad draftsmanship, but in the majority of instances the legislative purpose is simply to lay down a general standard capable of serving as a guide and of being adjusted to meet changing conditions and practices.

Our task as law students, judges, and lawyers is to discover the legislative intention. We approach our task by looking at the whole statute and by observing the problem with which the legislature set out to cope (found in committee hearings, reports, investigations, and the like) and the ideas which the legislature expressed in debating the proper solution to the problem. Over a long period of time, certain rules have been developed for dealing with this matter. The whole question is presided over by the guides of common sense, reference to past experience, and a sort of sizing up of the historical events which led up to the statute. To say only this much is perhaps tantalizing, but to say more would be to say too much on a complex subject.

Administrative Orders and Regulations

Today's practicing lawyer knows that the law rules are found not only in the decided cases and the statutes but also in the rules, regulations, orders, and decisions of the state and federal administrative agencies. He is frequently called upon, in drawing up a trust fund or in disposing of property for a client, to give advice concerning the latest regulations of the Collector of Internal Revenue. In setting up any corporate structure, the lawyer must of necessity take into consideration the effect of the orders and regulations of the Securities and Exchange Commission as well as the latest tax regulations. Landlords as well as tenants seek advice as to the effect of the regulations controlling rents. Importers and exporters desire information about the rulings of the tariff commission and the interpretations of the antitrust laws. Manufacturers want advice as to the regulations of the Federal Trade Commission and of the Food and Drug Administration as well as the orders of the National Labor Relations Board. Companies engaged in the production and marketing of petroleum and its products must be advised as to the various state and federal regulations on the conservation of natural resources. These are but a few of the possible examples. In order for the lawyer to give such advice, it is not sufficient that he search the cases and statutes. He must search for the law rules among the orders, regulations, and instructions of the agencies involved.

Custom as a Source of Law Rules

These, then, are the traditionally accepted sources of the law rules; but there are others which are less generally accepted. One of these latter is custom. This is sometimes referred to as ways of doing things which have obtained from "time immemorial" or which have been followed "since the memory of man runneth not to the contrary." By those writers who maintain that law only exists when courts declare it or legislatures enact it, custom as a source of law is either denied or confined to an irreducible minimum. To those who maintain that, after all, law usually contents itself with preserving the customary methods of behavior wherever possible, custom is of great importance as the original source of law which courts and legislatures merely declare but do not create. This is an interesting debate, which you will pursue in courses such as jurisprudence and international law. However, in an age of great legislative activity, the area of customary law is inclined to wane. It is not to be denied that early law and the formative period of international law leaned heavily upon custom.

Doctrinal Writings

Still another debated source of law rules, long accepted in international law and in the civil law countries as evidence of what the law is, but only slowly gaining acceptance in common-law jurisdictions, is doctrinal writing. Such is found in the form of textbooks, commentaries, law review articles, or restatements. In the civil law, it is well known that Justinian, in his famous codification of Roman law, laid great emphasis upon the writings of certain jurists and that the writings of Domat and Pothier had great influence on the content and development of the *Code Napoléon* of France.

The continental lawyer refers to and uses the works of commentators as naturally as the Anglo-American lawyer uses decided cases. In international law, the works of Grotius, Vattel, and Pufendorf, to name but a few, formed solid cores around which grew much of the substance of international law until the late nineteenth century. In the common law, the names of certain writers appear frequently in the briefs and reports of cases, men such as Glanvil, Bracton, Littleton, Coke, Blackstone, Kent, Story, and Benjamin, and in more recent years the names of Williston, Wigmore, Pollock, Holmes, and Winfield. Today, references to the Restatements of the Law, prepared by the American Law Institute, appear regularly in the court reports, although their authority rests upon the eminence of the men who wrote them and the soundness of the reasoning displayed.

It must be recognized that with the rapid increase in the number of statutes and reported cases, and the apparent impossibility of one man's reading and learning them all, both lawyers and courts have come to refer more and more to the works and compilations of authors who have devoted themselves to an exhaustive study of limited segments of the law territory. Unless through some miracle the number and mass of statutes, orders, and reported cases become less or man's ability to read and comprehend becomes vastly improved, the use of these so-called "secondary sources" or "reference books" is likely to increase.

Natural Law

The most controversial source of law rules we have saved for last, and admittedly our discussion is sketchy. This is the natural law or, as some call it, the law of nature. There are many definitions of natural law, and any definition here given is likely to offend some authority. Briefly, the posi-

tion of the natural law school is that anterior to all positive
law there exists a law of nature, that this law is universal
and unchanging, that it is discoverable in part by reason,
and that positive or man-made law more or less approximates
or approaches natural law, depending upon the perfection of
reason in discovering it.   An illustration of natural law as
a source is found in the Louisiana Civil Code, which by article
21 provides that "in all civil matters, where there is no express
law, the judge is bound to proceed and decide according to
equity.   To decide equitably, an appeal is to be made to
natural law and reason, or received usages, where positive
law is silent."

The idea of a pre-existing, perfect, universal law of nature
which man can discover at least in part through the use of
reason has captivated the fancy of legal philosophers and
judges throughout the ages.   Opposed to it is the idea that
there is no law except positive law, and that to admit the idea
of pre-existing, undeclared law would be to open the door to
arbitrary and capricious acts of men and judges for which
they would claim foundation in natural law.   You will be
made aware of this controversy in your course in constitutional law when you discuss "inalienable rights" and "due
process" and in your course in tort when you refer to the
"reasonable man" doctrine.   To say more about the matter
would be to say too much for the scope of this book.   The
available literature is immense and includes such famous
names as Plato, Aristotle, Aquinas, Suarez, Grotius, and
Hooker.

These, then, are the principal sources of the law rules:
the cases, the statutes, and the administrative orders and regulations.   To these we have added custom, doctrinal writings,
and natural law.   It is a vast territory.   The extent to which
one penetrates it depends upon the problem at hand, and

the patience of the searcher.   The territory is not fixed and immutable.   It is changing as man's needs change.   In the long view, law rules are but the tools with which to accomplish the task.   When they cease to be considered as tools and are looked at as ends in themselves, history teaches us that they are eventually relegated to a museum of "oddities in the law."   It is a wise carpenter who abandons a tool when he discovers that it no longer performs its function.

12

MAKING THE INFORMED GUESS

The Lawyer as a Predictor

The man who knows what the legal problem is, who knows the facts pertaining to it, and who has the applicable law rules in hand can proceed to advise his client as to the best course of action to be taken. From his knowledge of past and present, he "guesses" into the future. The difference between this and other guesses is that it is an informed guess based upon a calculated risk. The cabinet maker to whom you take lumber and state that you desire him to make a table for you, looks at the wood, calculates what his tools will do, and tells you whether or not he can create for you a table. The lawyer to whom you take a problem examines the facts and proofs, recalls and studies his tools, the law rules, and advises you on the course of action to be taken and the probabilities of success.

Lawyers, like other men, cannot guarantee the future for their clients, but they must be prepared to guess as to that future. They can only look carefully at all the probabilities, weigh them, and advise on the basis of what they see. The crux of the matter lies in being able to see with trained eyes, and trained eyes come with experience and practice. That is why as law students you must be trained not only to learn the law rules but also to use them and to know what they can accomplish. The artist is judged not by the tools which he knows or possesses but by how he uses them.

There are many ways in which you will be trained to use these tools. For example, your instructor will devote much time to setting for you hypothetical cases upon which you must work and come up with an answer. This gives you a chance to apply the rules which you have learned and to test, against his questioning, the results which you obtain. Then, too, the law school provides moot cases upon which you will be expected to prepare briefs and argument. These moots consist of stated facts which you must analyze for yourself. One of the most important opportunities for you to display the use of the rules occurs in the examinations which consist principally of stated fact-situations to which you will be expected to apply the law rules as you know and understand them. Of course, these are but simulations of real practice, but they provide an acceptable challenge to your best efforts.

Reducing the Margin of Error

There is no denying the old adage that experience is the best teacher, and it is true that law schools can provide only a minimum of training in this field. However, certain points can and will be made in your law training which can be emphasized here. We begin with certain truisms. The value of any prediction is measured by whether or not it ultimately proves sound. All predictions as to future events are open to error. Even the famous sayings of the Delphic oracle required some strained interpretations to keep the record clear. The old saying that one can safely predict only that which has already happened is quite true. In the face of these difficulties, the lawyer can only attempt to make the most informed guess possible, reducing the margin of error as far as is intelligently possible. He may well find that the trust settlement which he drew to last for ten years is set at naught before half the time has passed by a court decision reversing an earlier case upon which he had relied in his advice.

Thus, to the best of his ability, the lawyer must take into account the possibilities of change, in the sense of watching the "trends." Lawyers, like doctors and other scientists, come to qualify their predictions or, as some say, "hedge" or "engage in double talk," which sometimes infuriates clients who wish certainty. In the long run, these qualifications often give a more accurate picture upon which to take action. Then, too, the hypothesis or informed guess should be considered a tentative one, until it has been satisfactorily proved. These guesses must often be reshaped in the light of newly discovered evidence. They must be checked again and again. This is the method of the sound lawyer. There is always the temptation, once the hypothesis survives the first few tests, to equate it with truth and stop checking. Then, instead of looking at the problem, we look at our preconception of the problem, and not infrequently the mote in our eye prevents us from seeing truly. Many a man who assumed that of course there was gasoline in his motorcar has gone to great pains to seek mechanical defects, only to find that the real problem was the lack of fuel. The picture of a full gasoline tank blinded him to the fact of an empty one.

Defending Your Guess

For you, as a law student, the real challenge comes not in making the informed guess but in defending it. When you have answered the question set in class or on examination by proposing a course of legal action to be taken, the next question is inevitably: Why? Guesses can be made by hunch, coin-flipping, intuition, or a quick glance at last year's notes. But informed guesses imply that the guess is based upon demonstrable evidence and has been reached by a method which stands up under analysis. The instructor wants to know not only that you have the proper tools but also that you can use them in a proper manner. The chemistry instructor who gives to the student an unknown to identify is of course interested in knowing that it is properly named, but he is also interested in knowing the method by which the student proceeded to test and discover the nature of the unknown. The man who has acquired a method knows how and where to attack problems. If the method be unsound, the results are not likely to escape that defect.

The Importance of Method

We have now completed our glance at the legal method of analysis and synthesis. We have seen that in large measure it follows the scientific method, and yet it has certain variations made necessary by the particular task which it is to perform, namely, the application of value judgments. There are those in the law schools who would disagree with the emphasis which we have placed upon the method of analysis, but the fact remains that it is our traditional method. It is not too much to say that knowledge of method is the most important thing which you will carry away from your law school training. It is unlikely that you will remember even the names of more than a few of the cases studied or the particulars of the statutes. These you can always look up again as occasion demands. But the method of approach to problems, old and new, the method of testing them against experience and logic, this you can acquire in law school. This is the hard core of the matter. The remainder is by and large the application of method to specific areas of experience.

13

TECHNIQUES OF ARGUMENT

Lawyers are traditionally supposed to be masters of the art of argument and debate. How many generations of students have studied the orations of Cicero, the lawyer of Rome, as masterpieces of persuasion! In our own country, the names of Webster, Clay, and Calhoun, and in England the names of Burke and Lord Birkenhead stand as peaks of eminence in this field. The simple persuasive power of Lincoln's address at Gettysburg stands as a model for many lesser lights. For the lawyer in litigation must persuade the court of the soundness of the solution which he urges. As we remarked earlier, the physician himself assumes final control of his patient's cure, but the lawyer can only urge his client's claim upon a court, which has the final control through its power to decide. Thus, although the medical student needs no such training in the techniques of argument and persuasion, it is part and parcel of the equipment of the lawyer.

Increased Emphasis on Argumentative Techniques

Not too long ago, neither lawyers nor law schools spoke of such a matter as "argumentative techniques." In fact, there are still circles in which the use of the word "technique" in connection with law is thought to indicate something overly-clever and inclined to be "sharp." It was of course known that some lawyers were "wizards" with a jury, that some were most sought after in trial work, and that others were extremely effective before appellate courts. But there was little attempt to study the arts used by them in achieving their results. Occasionally, some of the more famous of them, such as Darrow or Lord Birkenhead, wrote memoirs or popular treatises in which they related their experiences, and younger lawyers and law students would pore over them with or without recommendation from others. Still others visited courts and saw their favorites in action, noting their manner, dress, voice, timing and histrionics. But to study the matter formally was considered either impossible or perhaps undignified. All of this occurred in that period in which salesmen and actors learned only through apprenticeship and not through courses in such skills and arts.

Even today there is by no means general agreement on the proposition that these things can be taught. The influence of the psychologist and the professional educator has been felt, but has also met opposition. However, many law schools are paying increased attention to this problem as a rewarding approach to law study. Its use is being explored in such courses as trial practice, procedure, and evidence. The apparent notion behind this emphasis is that it is the function of a lawyer in a law suit to convince the court of the validity of his client's contentions and that therefore all the persuasive arts and techniques should be studied to further this end. It is apparently further based upon the notion that judges and jurors are real people like ourselves, with likes and dislikes, pet notions, and prejudices, and are therefore subject to the persuasive arts.

To the layman (unless he be perchance the client) and to the philosophical jurist, this concept of the lawyer's rôle leaves several questions answered unsatisfactorily. It may

well be asked: But is it not the rôle of the lawyer to see that
justice is done?   Laymen have always asked: Does this mean
that the lawyer will argue the case even though he believes
that his client is morally wrong?   Men have long debated
these questions and many answers have been propounded.
Some reply that there is no such thing as absolute justice, but
only relative justice, which in our system is achieved by
having an impartial court decide between the contentions of
litigants before it.   Others answer that these are questions of
ethics which do not concern the lawyer as a lawyer, but only
as an individual man.   Still others say that it is no more the
lawyer's rôle to see that justice is done than it is the baker's or
the grocer's; that the lawyer is merely the agent to conduct
a given transaction; that he merely carries out the wishes of
others.   Perhaps there are no completely satisfactory answers
to these profound questions.   In practice, the lawyer is bound
by his oath, taken on becoming a member of the bar, to uphold
the laws and to abide by the canons of ethics of his profession.
The real answer lies in the integrity of each man, in his conscience, even more than it resides in the group ethics of the
profession.   The man who holds that action is responsive to
ideals will attempt to see justice done for his client.   We
know little of the struggles which go on in a man's inner self
as he strives to know what justice is for his client.   We know
many of the occasions when men err and stray, because the
evil has a way of getting shouted from the housetops, while
the good is "oft interred with their bones."

Let us assume, however, that there is a reasonable doubt
as to the just result in a certain case, and since the tools of
argument are available to the just and unjust alike, let us proceed to examine them.   We shall, however, confine ourselves
to an introduction to those tools of argument which you will
met in your law studies.   While we have referred to them

as tools to be used in court argument, yet you will be given an opportunity to observe and use them in class discussion, moot court, term papers, law review writing, and examinations. You will also probably find that you are already familiar with them from your undergraduate study, or from your own experience, whether derived from persuading your father that you ought to have the car, or convincing an instructor that you really knew the material of a course despite your poor showing on the examination.

The Difference in Approaches to Legal Problems

It is axiomatic that there are many approaches to a problem. It is also axiomatic that, given man's fallibilities, all the approaches do not lead to the same solution or explanation. Some men approach problems from a cold, careful analytical point of view. Some tackle a problem from the point of view of the historical development leading up to and finding expression in the problem. Some approach a problem from the point of view of its place in the whole functioning of society. Some see in the attack on each problem a search for underlying purpose. Each approach has its staunch adherents. Each approach has its particular methods, tests, and rules. Although it is probable that no one of these approaches in itself holds the whole key to a problem, yet each performs a useful function.

Legal thinkers, whether they have been judges, teachers, writers, or lawyers, have given great thought to the approach to legal problems. They have sought to explain the phenomenon of law itself and to create out of its whole activity an understandable system. The quest is by no means over or settled. Men still probe into the frontiers of law and come up with new ideas. The impact of these ideas is felt by both judge and legislator. That which we are about to do is to show the use of these great ideas in action.   We will call them "approaches" and consider them separately, but once again the warning is given that the divisions are arbitrary and that in practice the arguments usually make use of one or more of the approaches in combination.

The Analytical or Logical Approach

To those who consider law as the embodiment of the perfect use of reason, and they are a distinguished company, this technique of argument is most important.   Essentially, it is the application of logic to legal argument on the assumption that the argument which presents the soundest logic will convince the court and prevail.   This approach, as is to be expected, lays great stress upon precise terminology, exact references, and adherence to categories.   The English jurist John Austin (1790–1859) is the leading figure in the so-called analytical school of jurisprudence.   In this country, Wesley N. Hofeld (1879–1918) undertook the monumental task of attempting to analyze the fundamental legal conceptions so as to permit exactness of legal speech and writing.   There is little need to go further in setting forth the general features of this approach.   It must be sufficient to set forth a few of the major techniques which distinguish it in argument.

Perhaps the first to come to mind is the technique of *distinguishing a case on its facts.*   Let us assume that in the case which you are arguing, the opposing counsel has cited a leading case which he contends should control the decision in your case.   Assume further that the cited case contains facts *A*, *B*, and *C*, all of which facts are present in your case.   Now assume that your case also contains fact *D*, which was not present in or referred to in the cited case.   Here an attempt can be made to distinguish your case from that cited, on the basis that the presence of fact *D* makes the cases different and, since they are materially different, the same result need not follow.   This exercise is the one with which you will become most familiar in class, usually in the form of the questions: How do you distinguish these cases? or Why did the court reach a different result in this case from the one which we have just discussed?

A further technique is that of *distinguishing a case on the law*.   For example, let us assume that in argument the opposing counsel has cited a case decided by the highest court of a neighboring state, which reaches a result contrary to your position.   Let us further assume that the facts in the cited case and those in your case cannot be distinguished.   If you can find that the case cited against you was decided in reliance upon a statute of that state, and that your state does not possess such a statute, then the argument can be made that the two cases can be distinguished in that a statutory command was present in one case but not in the other.   Or, again, suppose that there is urged against you a leading case decided by the highest court of your own jurisdiction.   Assume that the facts are similar.   If you can find that the case urged against you was decided on a point of law raised by the pleadings—for example, that the court did not have jurisdiction over one of the parties—but not on the merits, then you have a basis for distinguishing the two cases, in that the decision is not controlling on the merits.   Or suppose that since the earlier decision, the legislature has changed the applicable law by statute.   You will be trained in this technique by such means as the insertion in your case-book of old cases decided under procedure no longer in effect, and instructions to speculate on how each case might be decided under modern code pleading.

This approach is useful not only to distinguish cases, but also as a means for *extending a case by analogy to reach a desired result*. Let us assume that there is a leading case in your jurisdiction which holds that a contract with an insane person will not be enforced, for the expressed reason that the insane person does not possess the requisite intelligence required to enter into contractual relations. Now assume further that you are involved in a case in which enforcement of a contract is sought against your client, who is not insane but is mentally deficient and possesses the mentality of a child of four years. Further assume that no case has been found in your jurisdiction upon the precise point of the responsibility or capacity of a mentally deficient person. The argument can be made that since the court has decided that an insane person should not be bound because he lacked the requisite intelligence to contract, then by analogy the mentally deficient person who has only the mentality of a child of four years should not be bound, for the same reasons. Thus, by applying the court's own reasoning, we urge upon it consistency in an analogous situation. You will recognize your training in this technique when your instructor phrases a question somewhat in this fashion: "On the basis of the case just discussed, what would be your opinion as to the result if we changed the facts thus?" or "Since the court has decided this point as to corporations, would it also apply to cooperatives?" This process of argument is particularly useful where statutes are involved in which are contained enumerations of examples plus a statement saying that the listing is not complete but is to include objects of a like nature.

A contrary technique to the one just discussed may be illustrated by *extending a case by analogy to reach a criticised result.* Here let us assume that opposing counsel is contending for a position and it is difficult to deny that such would be a defensible solution for this case for this client. However, if the court were so to decide in this case, then the question may be asked as to the effect of such a decision upon other similar cases. We extend the principle upon which this decision would be based so far that eventually it is reduced to an absurd position. Thus we argue that the court should not so decide this case, because such a decision would open the door to later results which could not be defended. This argument is often phrased: "If the plaintiff is allowed to recover on this claim, then the courts will be swamped by litigants taking up the valuable time of the courts with ill-grounded suits" or "If the decision in this case goes in favor of the government, then no private business man is safe from fishing expeditions into his private affairs at the whim of any agency." Some writers have called this the "What are we coming to?" argument, or the "parade of horribles." You will note in some of your cases the court's reaction to such an argument when it, despite the argument, decides the case as opposing counsel suggests, noting that the decision is to turn on its particular facts and is not to be regarded as stating a general rule or precedent. In law school, your training in this technique may well be painful when the instructor takes your answer to his posed question and by analogy pushes you farther and farther from the main case until your position becomes absurd. Socrates was a master at this technique, and the rest of us are but poor imitators.

The most usual form of this approach is the argument that *like situations should be disposed of similarly.* This is the much-used argument of the "case on all fours," which is used by the lawyer who has found what he believes to be an exactly similar case decided by the same court or by a court superior to the one in which he is urging his case. The argument is essentially this: This point of law has been decided before in this state, and the decision there given controls this case since the facts are similar. It is the old argument of logical consistency. To realize its power, you have only to read some of the comments written when the Supreme Court of the United States reverses itself on a matter previously decided.

The counter-argument to this position usually phrases itself in some variation of Emerson's remark about <u>consistency as the hobgoblin of little minds,</u> or the old adage that two wrong decisions do not make a right one. The best counter-argument is of course that the all-fours case is a rarity and that "all-fourness" must be demonstrated. You will be introduced to this argument in many ways: in your class discussion, in your study of the concepts of precedent, *stare decisis*, and *ratio decidendi*, in your moot court cases, and occasionally when your instructor sets a question upon which there has been a recent court decision.

Many variations of these arguments could be cited, but we will mention only one more. <u>It might be characterized by some such tag as *words of wise men all remind us*.</u> Despite the great number of cases decided each year by the various courts, you will find that the court in your jurisdiction has not been called upon to pass upon all the legal questions which man conjures up. You may find that although the court before which you come has not passed upon the question, yet courts of other states have done so in a manner favorable to your client's contention. Hence you will cite to your court some decisions from other courts and urge it to follow the same line of thought. This can be dangerous as well as helpful. Some courts do not wish to appear to be following other courts, preferring to exercise their own independent judgment. Others give careful attention to the decisions of other courts on the assumption that legal ideas are a common heritage and no one jurisdiction has a monopoly on reason.

Perhaps enough has been said to illustrate a few of the most frequently used arguments which can be gathered around this analytical or logical approach. You will find many more of them as you study your courses in procedure and evidence. They will be particularly evident in the old common-law pleading, which was to some the perfection of the logician's art. Again, it is well to remember that what we have just done is not by any means to discuss and explain the analytical school of jurisprudence. That will be done in your courses in jurisprudence and legal theory. What we have done is to apply that method of thinking about law to the particular function of argument. As you read your cases, watch for illustrations of these techniques in the court's opinion as they distinguish and apply cases and extend old holdings by analogy to reach new results.

The Approach through History

It is a truism, too often neglected in thought, that history did not begin when we entered on its stage nor is it likely to end when we depart. Our period is but one act in a long continuous drama. So, too, our laws and our decisions are but a small part of the evolution of law. Each case that is decided is a part of that growth. Hence to many legal writers and great judges a clear reference to history is a vital part of every decision. To them the problem before the judge is not an isolated phenomenon; it is part of a whole development. To them the decision of a legal problem can best be made by tracing its roots into the past so that the present manifestation can be understood and dealt with in the light of its history.

The so-called historical school of jurisprudence contains many famous names. In England, it was espoused by such men as the great Maitland, Sir Frederick Pollock, Sir Henry Maine, and Sir Paul Vinogradoff. On the continent, its great exponent was Friedrich Karl von Savigny. In this country,

Professor Wigmore has done much to indicate its importance. Again, as you read your cases, you will come to know the judges who dig deep into the history of the problem about which they are to decide. Some of their opinions read like papers on legal history, and one can appreciate how carefully they seek to integrate their opinions into all that has gone before, so that one senses not so much an exercise in logic as a feeling of historical growth. Here then is a second approach to the argument and decision of a case in which we can note certain techniques.

The most powerful of these arguments is the position that *the case must be viewed in its historical setting.* For example, let us assume that a case is urged against you as controlling precedent which was decided by a court of last resort a hundred years ago on facts similar to those of your case. The opposing counsel may rely heavily upon the logical approach of consistency, contending that lapsed time does not affect the logical validity of the proposition. It is up to you to dig into the history of that period for the setting of the earlier case. It may be possible to show that certain factors which made the decision acceptable in the light of conditions of that day are not now present and that intervening events render such a decision out of keeping with the modern legal developments. You have perhaps heard the phrase "horse and buggy law" applied to decisions which were seemingly reached without regard to the fact that we now live in a motorized era. You will undoubtedly be well indoctrinated in this approach in law school, since instructors in law frequently sketch in the historical background of the cases which are discussed. Law review articles and comments likewise concern themselves with placing the new cases into the historic fabric of the law.

A further use of the historical approach in argument is

illustrated by the statement that a decision in your client's favor is in line with the *trend of the jurisprudence.* For example, let us assume that the position for which you are contending has not yet been taken by any court in a decided case, but that on the basis of your study and observation of existing decisions it would appear that the law is developing in the direction of your position. This argument is similar to the extension by analogy argument discussed earlier, but the emphasis is upon historical continuity rather than upon logic. Your argument will consist of a careful résumé of the earlier cases, indicating a step-by-step movement toward your position, supported by the opinions of legal historians, doctrinal writings, and the dicta of judges. This is one of the important uses of dicta. You will become quite familiar with the term "trend" in your study of law, since lawyers are coming to use it almost as frequently as economists.

There is also the useful argument that a decision in your client's favor will *bring the problem in line with developments in related fields.* It is a common mistake, as Professor Toynbee has pointed out, to assume that history is always something which happened in the remote past and that it hasn't happened to us now for some time. Maitland's celebrated phrase "the seamless web of history" includes the present. We can observe the relationships among events of our own times and so use the argument of history to preserve the fabric from unsightly tears. As Maitland reminds us, "today we study the day before yesterday in order that yesterday may not paralyse to-day, and to-day may not paralyse to-morrow." The argument here referred to concerns the interdependence of all fields of action in the unity of history. In your courses in corporation law and in sales you will probably be referred to the writers on economics, marketing, and finance in order to see the areas of agreement and disagreement between the legal and economic solutions or patterns of thought.

A variation on the first argument about placing the case in its historical setting may be expressed in the phrase: *other times—other ways.* The story of history is one of a record of change, sometimes gradual, sometimes rapid. From Heraclitus to Bergson we have been reminded that we cannot step twice into the same river. Fortunes were once made in the manufacture of shoe buttons and horse collars, whereas today there is little market for such products. The beauty of the argument of history is that it does not prescribe a static world; in fact it does not always describe a logical one. If you glance at the statute books, there you will discover, extant and unrepealed, old laws which have long since outlived their usefulness as responses to the challenge which called them forth. Statutes in some states still provide fines imposed on those who travel on the Sabbath except on errands of mercy. Occasionally these are enforced and the people protest and legislatures act to repeal them as no longer in accord with life as we know it. Likewise, there exist decisions, reported and never expressly overruled, which no longer apply to the modern scene, for example, decisions setting forth the rights of women prior to their being granted equal rights with men. Here, then, is the argument that the lessons of history should be made use of so that law may grow to meet the needs and challenges of the age in which it is being made.

There is of course the counter-argument that, rightly or wrongly, *this case has been decided by the history books.* For example, where all the previously decided cases on a particular legal point add up to a single result in favor of your client and yet the result has been roundly criticised and reluctantly followed, this argument is sometimes used to assure the court that it is not its fault that it must follow a bad decision. On the one side is the heavy hand of the past; on the other is the attacking hand of the present. As you read your cases, watch for the courts which say that were this a case of first impression they might decide it differently, yet they feel bound to follow the past decisions. Sometimes they will couple this with the remark that if the law is to be changed, it is up to the legislature to do so.

The arguments from history can take many forms. These are but a few scattered examples. You will note others as you read your cases, or as you turn to the legislative history of a statute to seek its meaning. The judge who thinks in terms of history or who feels that the eyes of history are upon him will understand these arguments. Prior to the middle of the last century, it might be said that the logical-analytical and the historical approaches and the resulting argumentative techniques comprised almost exclusively the kit of the practicing lawyer. The past hundred years have seen the fashioning of new approaches and techniques which we now turn to discuss. In a way, however, it is perhaps sounder to say that these are not new techniques. We have merely given formal names and wider currency to some very old methods of argument.

The Approach through Sociology

Many men have not been content to view a legal problem narrowly as a set of legal propositions or as a result of historical forces. They have insisted that law is made by people for people and that the problems which people have are not solved by calling them either logical or historical maladjustments. The roster of names in the so-called sociological school of jurisprudence, like those in the other schools, is highly distinguished, but we will content ourselves with naming Roscoe Pound, formerly dean of the Harvard Law School, as it most active exponent. His writings have been received with deference both here and abroad.

To the sociological jurist, the problems with which the law concerns itself are social problems, of men acting with relation to one another in society. Therefore, they point out that the judge and lawyer should be trained in the understanding of social problems and that they should study and use the findings of the sociologists whenever they are applicable to the case before them. The ultimate result, it is said by some, would perhaps be that the lawyer would become a better sociologist than the sociologist himself and that law would become the highest form of applied sociology. Laying such claims aside for the moment, we should note that the importance of this approach is that it turns our attention to the study of man in his relations in society in order that law may deal intelligently with these relations as they are and not as they logically should be. There is no doubt that the concerted attacks of sociologists and jurists upon certain areas of law, such as juvenile court administration, penal reforms, domestic relations, and some aspects of tort law, have produced notable results. It is also true that lawyers, while reluctant to become sociologists as well, have nevertheless recognized in the sociological approach growing merit, and have used the approach functionally in argument. We will note two of the examples most frequently encountered.

One of these is the argument that *society does not act that way*. It is of course well known that the British drive their motorcars on the left-hand side of the road and Americans drive on the right, and that the rules of the road of the respective countries sanction this practice. Further, it is evident that confusion and clamor would result if the laws of one country in this matter were applied to the other. Visitors from one country or the other have attempted with little success to assert the logical rightness of one or the other method. We also know that many towns have ordinances providing a speed limit of ten or fifteen miles per hour, and that some enforce it, while others retain it as a nostalgic reminder of the way people used to act. We are also aware that one of the arguments for the retention of capital punishment is that it acts as a deterrent to other potential criminals, a contention disputed by other reasonable men. These are the more obvious examples.

Now let us assume that there has been urged against your contention a case which states in the opinion that the transaction of instalment buying is commonly done in a certain manner and that therefore doing it in another manner will not create an enforceable contract. Assume further that your research shows that in fact in the area in which the disputed transaction took place, the common manner of instalment buying is that which your client used and not that relied upon in the earlier case. Your argument then proceeds that since in the earlier case the court intended to approve the method in common use, the present court must first ascertain the method in common use at this time and not at some earlier period. To apply the earlier decision would be to approve the uncommon use and to create confusion and uncertainty in ordinary business transactions. You will discover some interesting examples of the operation of this approach and the conflicting results in the cases involving the so-called "attractive nuisance" doctrine in tort as applied to infant trespassers. The reluctance with which some courts have recognized that small children are "natural wanderers" rather than deliberate trespassers either argues that judges are unobservant parents or that even if children are natural wanderers they should not be. A prime example in this country of a law which had to give way in the face of popular reaction and refusal to obey was the prohibition law.

The argument may also be used in the sense of asserting that *this is the way in which society acts*. Assume that you have a legal problem upon which courts have not yet passed. Suppose that your study and research show that the normal societal behavior-pattern is that which your client has followed. It is then possible to argue that in the absence of any express prohibition of such conduct by legislative authority or any violation of good morals, the normal pattern of conduct should be approved. This argument is based upon two assumptions: that the way people act is relevant to what the law should be as to their actions where such is not dangerous to society; and that where the law bears a reasonable relationship to the habit pattern of the majority of the people, it will be more easily enforced and more readily obeyed.

The Approach through Economics

Just as the sociologist sometimes feels that law muddles up his special bailiwick of study unscientifically, so too the economist often asserts that lawyers would act more intelligently if they only knew something about economics. This has led some writers to maintain that a prime approach to legal problems is by way of economics. The economic determinist would probably assert that it is the sole approach. Since a great portion of law is concerned with such matters as rent, taxation, negotiable instruments, contracts, sales, insurance, corporate finance and management, regulation of business, and the like, all of which are matters of direct concern to the economist, it was inevitable that the disciplines of law and economics would overlap.

It is certainly desirable for the lawyer to know the work

of the economists in these fields, and the economist must take into account the legal regulations. This has made for closer and closer cooperation between the two fields. For example, the tax lawyer and the tax accountant, however much they may dispute as to their respective areas of exclusive interest, have been able to work together. This has been true also of the trust lawyers and the investment bankers. In recent years law schools have added courses in legal accounting and corporate finance, which action bears testimony to this mutual interest.

Out of this attempted integration of law and economics have come many techniques of argument, but it is believed that essentially they are all variations on one theme, namely, *let us look at the facts.* When Mr. Justice Holmes wrote down his now famous statement that "the life of the law has not been logic; it has been experience," he may well have laid the groundwork not only for his history of the common law, but also for all the experiential approaches as well.

But it is to another member of the Supreme Court of the United States, Mr. Justice Brandeis, that we usually accord the distinction of having introduced economic facts into court argument on a large scale. Brandeis, as an eminent corporation counsel, incorporated economic theory and findings so skilfully into his briefs and argument that we still refer to briefs which contain such materials as "Brandeis briefs." By the careful and persuasive coupling of economic statistics with legal argument, he was able to indicate in many instances the wide discrepancies between what business firms actually did and what the law assumed that they did.

Whether the argument be phrased in the form of a statement that "to do so would be to decide this case on the basis of the economics of 1860" or "we must be guided in such matters by the opinions of the experts in this field" or "to decide that way would be to ignore the real problem," the argument is always "Let us look at the facts." In other words, let us become as informed as we can in this matter so that we can reach a decision which will help to solve the problem and not simply to make it more confused and bewildering. It should also be noted that courts are not alone in having felt the impact of economic argument; legislatures too feel the full impact of statistics and reports in their lawmaking. As you come to learn about the administrative agencies, such as the Federal Trade Commission, you will discover that much of their work lies in the field of economic theory.

You will observe in your case-books on public utilities, corporate reorganization, and taxation a wider use of economic materials for study purposes. In the cases themselves, you will find evidence that courts are looking at economic facts in the forms of statistics, balance sheets, and all the stock-in-trade of the economist. You will also note in your cases in corporation law how often the court will state that it indulges a presumption in favor of the good faith of management, since courts are not economic experts and cannot substitute their judgment for that of management. It is also interesting to note that some other courts feel no such hesitation.

The argument from economics requires real work and much digging. As in law, the economists are not always in agreement, and the evidence upon which they base their "expertise" is baffling to the novice. But in a world in which law and economic theory are becoming increasingly intertwined, the argument "Let us look at the facts" is a most useful one. This is one of the opportunities to make use of your undergraduate training in such matters, because the lawyer who understands economic theory and practice as well as law may render his client invaluable aid. Looking at the facts is of course the first step; understanding them as well carries you by seven league boots toward the goal.

Other Modern Approaches

The past quarter-century has seen the battle of the spokesmen for what they term new approaches to law. The voices are by no means in accord, and there is little to be gained here in attempting to unscramble them, even if such could be done. Following the propensity for giving labels, some have called these new approaches by such names as "the realist school" and "the functional school," while some apply the term "pragmatist," and some refer to the "gastronomic school of jurisprudence" in "tribute" to the emphasis which some of the writers lay on what the judge had for breakfast before coming to court.

It is certainly unwise at this date to list any particular men as leading exponents of one or more of these approaches. You can, however, acquaint yourselves with some of the ideas by reading such works as Judge Frank's *Law and the Modern Mind*, Karl Llewellyn's *The Bramble Bush*, Thurman Arnold's *The Symbols of Government*, Edwin Robinson's *Law and the Lawyers*, and the law review articles of Walton Hamilton, Dean Wesley Sturges, and Mr. Justice Douglas. Much of the controversy stimulated by these writings has now simmered down as the ideas have become accepted or have been discarded, but the battle was an interesting and important one.

If we attempt to examine these various approaches with a view to pulling from them any general threads of emphasis, the following would stand out. All of these schools of thought seem to have been greatly influenced by the findings of the psychologist and psychiatrist, or the anthropologist and social scientist. All of them seem to emphasize the concept that law has a definite function to perform in society and that this function is capable of being studied scientifically. Most of them lay stress upon the notion that judges, in making judgments, are affected to some extent by their social, economic, and political backgrounds and predilections, and that consequently individual judges can be studied with a view to predicting their action on certain problems. These thoughts have led the proponents of the new approaches to place great stress upon techniques, method, procedure, and evidence as the most important elements of law school training. Finally, these new voices seem agreed upon concerted opposition to the concept of natural law.

From the point of view of argumentative techniques, a phrase which this school has made popular, one device should be mentioned which has had considerable influence. This may be described as *directing the argument to the predilections of the particular judge*. There is of course nothing new in this technique. Actors and public speakers have long been accustomed to "sense" the tone of their audiences and to direct their appeal to that interest. The advertising agent, the merchandiser, the public relations expert, the Hooper-raters, all have cultivated this technique, in that they have measured, cajoled, or "played-to" the people with whom they deal. The statistical studies of the "average man in the street," the "average listener," or the "average voter" now reach out and encompass the "average judge or juror."

In recent years there has been a sharp increase in the number of studies of judicial administration, *i.e.*, of the judicial records of certain judges and courts. These studies have been made on the state as well as the federal level. As would be expected, the Supreme Court of the United States has come in for closest scrutiny. Each new appointment to the court is a signal for an evaluation of the justice's past work and a cautious prediction as to his future opinions. Each year the work of the Supreme Court is carefully analyzed by law reviews, through noting trends and departures from earlier positions as well as providing an evaluation of specific decisions. Labels, such as "conservative," "liberal," and "reactionary," are applied without stint.

The importance of all this lies in the centering of attention on the notion that the argument is for the purpose of convincing the judges and juries, and that these are men and women who, in making decisions, are likely to give heed, consciously or unconsciously, to their past experiences and to the political, social, and economic views which they hold or which have been engrained into them. Hence, in arguing to them, you seek, in following this approach, to use their predilections when they are in your favor and to avoid calling them up when they are not. The insurance agent or motorcar salesman with a special policy or model for sale studies his "prospect" from every angle, and so directs his sales argument that it will play a melody and not a discord on his client's purse strings.

Baldly stated, it is this notion that some of the newer voices would apply to law. This aspect of manipulation, while based upon sound teachings of applied psychology, has in it the danger that, in unscrupulous hands, it may be used irresponsibly. One may question whether, in the rôle of mere technicians, lawyers will continue to hold the respected position they have attained. Here, as in so many other matters, there is both good and danger in the technique, depending upon the end for which it is used and the one who uses it.

The Approach through Purpose

We have reserved until last a discussion of this approach, not because it is the most recent (for in fact it can be traced back at least as far as Plato), but rather because it poses questions which strike at the whole of legal thought. There is a distinct cleavage between those who view law solely as a means and those who consider that part of law's function is the statement of ends. In other words, is law merely the means through which democracy functions or do the principles of democracy rest in and upon our organic law? Is law only the sum total of the laws, or does law include also the ends of social effort?

If law is viewed solely as a means, with no responsibility towards and no part in the statement of the ends which the means further, then law tends to become machinery and the lawyer's task comes to be viewed as the manipulation of that machinery. Those who hold this view would consider that a study of ends and purposes was the province of the philosopher or the political scientist and not a primary responsibility of the law school. At most they would place such a study among the upper-class elective seminars in law schools.

If, on the other hand, law and judges and lawyers are to be concerned with, and in a sense responsible for, the ends for which the means are used, then there is a great need for us to be seriously concerned in law study with the ends and aims of the society of which we are a part. There can be little doubt that those who drew up the Declaration of Independence and the Constitution considered not only that they were providing the means by which the new nation was to function but also that they were shaping and declaring the ends and purposes for which it was to stand. These men were lawmakers. It is surely no secret that the great judges, such as Mansfield, Ellesmere, Kent, Marshall, Story, Waite, Holmes, Brandeis, and Cardozo, to name but a few, considered that they bore a great responsibility for the shaping of the ends which the laws serve. It is likewise no secret that our great statesmen and legislators, charged with the responsibility of negotiating treaties and providing legislation, considered themselves answerable in the eyes of history for the aims and purposes they sought to state and preserve. No one can read the Constitution of the United States, the nineteenth century reform legislation in Great Britain, the so-called "New Deal" legislation of the thirties, or the Charter of the United Nations, without becoming aware that the statement of purpose is part and parcel with the words. This applies whether or not you agree with the purpose stated. Nor is it any secret that the great lawyers and advocates have consciously aided in the molding of purpose. Further, it is well known that the great legal writers of the common law, from Bracton to Pound, considered their writings to be something more than treatises on mechanics and manipulation.

Education in law, as we have pointed out before, exists to prepare men for service not only as lawyers, but as judges, legislators, statesmen, and administrators. For this reason, you will be introduced in your law training to the great ideas of the legal philosophers, statesmen, judges, and advocates. These are live ideas, still possessed of challenge, and it is part of your obligation and privilege to yourself to wrestle with them. There is still a special magic in them, and he who loses sight of it steps aside from the joy which can come through the study of law.

The value of the argument to purpose is a great one. It serves to check the individual instance against the general purpose. It may take the form of the argument of "public policy," "good faith," "sound morals," "private enterprise," "general welfare," "human rights," or the "democratic way of life," to name but a few. You need only to read the briefs, arguments, and opinions of some of the cases in constitutional law to appreciate the power of this argument. The intelligent use of this method requires that you yourself have thought through the whole problem of your case in its relation to the developing purpose of law.

It would be wrong to assume that we have exhausted either the approaches or the techniques of argument in this brief discussion. Even by the time you read this, man's ingenuity may have devised some new variation on these themes. Nor is it to be assumed that we have adequately set forth even the broadest outline of these great schools of jurisprudence. Law schools themselves can give little more than an outline of these ideas, because one lifetime is not enough in which to explore them.

The rôle of argument is to convey your point of view persuasively so that others may understand and accept it. The minds of no two men function exactly alike, and yet communication must be established between the lawyer and the judge, not only for conveying external facts of experience, but also for the transmission of ideas. In order to communicate ideas, it is first necessary that we have them clearly in our own minds, lest the static of our own unclear thinking blot out the ideas.

14

ALL'S WELL THAT TESTS WELL

No commentary, however small, which purports to treat of the study of law would be complete without some remarks on the subject of examinations.

Man's life has become a series of tests from the cradle to the grave, be it for allergies, intelligence, aptitude, or *rigor mortis*. Eventually, they tell us, we may all be reduced to a set of symbols on an IBM machine. In this matter of testing, law and medical schools bear the reputation of being excellent breeding grounds for stomach ulcers, insomnia, and caffeine nerves. Why this must be so, no one has ever explained, except to point out that life is like that. That it is so, we soon learn and accept or else become happy savages. For the purpose of the discussion which follows, we will assume that examinations are necessary evils.

The primary purpose of the examination is to ascertain, in as objective a fashion as possible, whether the student has understood the study-material sufficiently well to enable him to use this knowledge in solving legal problems set by the instructor. In law schools and in bar examinations, a secondary purpose which has been served is to weed out the unfit so that the profession will be protected against the incompetent practitioner and the public will not be injured. We can begin our discussion by making certain general remarks about law examinations.

The test of the knowledge is its use. This is of course merely a form of the old maxim that all knowledge is for use. The notion, sometimes held by beginning law students, that all the materials are simply to be memorized like so many dates in history and spouted back on the examination, ought to be eradicated for several reasons. Even if it were desirable to do so, it is impossible to memorize all the required materials. Mere memorization is not what is called for on the examinations, except perhaps in legal bibliography and some types of true-false examinations. The important thing is to marshal the essential knowledge, ready for use. This means that the materials must be digested rather than memorized. It means that you must practice the use of the tools so that they are not strange, awkward gadgets on the day of the examination.

No matter how many hours you have slaved over abstracting the required cases—no matter how faithfully you have attended class and copied down each pearl of wisdom—no matter how beautifully and neatly your notes are annotated in red and green inks—no matter how conscientiously you have read the outside cases—unless that material has been made a part of you as understood knowledge which you can use in solving examination problems, you may well fail to pass the examination or to do as well as you wish to do. For the ultimate test of knowledge is whether you can put it to work for you.

It is true that some memorization is helpful. To know the name of a leading case which is applicable to the problem at hand in the examination is to have a shorthand method of indicating your awareness of the case and its applicability without having to take up precious time in describing the facts. To know the section numbers of a statute, such as the Negotiable Instruments Law, is again a short way of referring to specific knowledge without the necessity of spelling it all out. Such memorizations are useful, but not essential.

There are many tried and useful methods for getting the knowledge into your head rather than simply into your notebook. Periodic review of the material you have already covered, in the light of the class discussion of these materials, paying particular attention to the hypothetical cases posed in class and the approaches taken to solving them, is very useful. This should be done at least once each week, while the material is still fresh in your mind. The construction of an outline or *précis* for each subject studied, composed of a digested version of the law on particular topics and gleaned from your briefs, notes, discussion, and outside reading, is particularly valuable where an examination is to cover the work of a whole year. Reading over old stale notes months after they have been taken consumes too much time as a method for studying for an examination. The outline should be brief enough to be covered in a day's hard review and complete enough to suggest but not develop the principal topics for which you are to be held responsible by the examiners. Thus in the final reviews those topics which are not clear to you can be developed by further research or reference to your notes.

Another method frequently used to advantage is that of group discussion of the problems which have been raised in the cases or in class. Several good heads are sometimes better than one. This is sometimes done as the basis for preparing an outline. It has the advantage of giving you experience in formulating your ideas orally and in writing. Sometimes, if the group is not well chosen, it has the disadvantage of slowing up your own study.

Still a further method often recommended by instructors is that of going over old examinations and testing your ability to make satisfactory answers to the problems there posed.

There is of course no one best way. Some men cannot study effectively in groups, and so work out their own methods of setting questions for themselves. There are of course ready-made outlines for sale, in most courses. Upperclassmen who have done well in former examinations frequently "make available" their study notes or outlines. But it must be remembered that the greatest value of an outline is making it and that no "canned" outline is a substitute for getting the matter into your head.

Law examinations are prepared on the assumption that you will practice law. Despite the fact that many men study law with no intention of entering into practice, but rather of using the legal education as a background for some other work, the examinations are prepared and marked on the assumption that a potential practitioner is being tested. Since the successful attainment of a law degree is in most instances the qualification for taking a bar examination and entering the practice, it is to be expected that law schools feel a high degree of responsibility for testing their students with practice in view. This means that the questions set are likely to consist of problems as nearly like those which might confront the practitioner as possible. Some instructors set as examination questions the facts of actual cases. Others, seeking a wider coverage, make up hypothetical cases raising more legal issues than would normally appear in an actual case. But, however the problem may be raised, you will be expected to make noises as nearly like a lawyer as possible.

Try to spot likely questions in advance. In those law schools in which the instructor in the course prepares and marks the examination, and this means most American law schools, it is frequently possible to detect the particular areas of the materials upon which he is likely to set questions. We said earlier that one school of jurisprudence lays great stress upon studying the particular judge or court before which your case is to be tried.   In law school you may get valuable training in this method by using the technique upon your instructor.   Observe which portions of the materials he lays particular stress upon, and those which he passes over with a broad comment.   By doing so, he may well be indicating his own evaluation of the materials and the respective difficulties of the topics involved.   Observe the type of hypothetical questions which he poses in class as well as the type of answers or approaches which he receives with the least disapproval.

This does not mean that it is always necessary to agree with the views of the instructor.   Frequently, instructors welcome disagreement, even on examinations, but it is always wise to know the instructor's views and to indicate that you know them, even when dissenting from them.   There are also times when the very manner of the instructor in developing a topic indicates a decided likelihood that he will be tempted to ask about it on the examination.   When all is said and done, there are only a certain number of topics in each course which present good problems for an examination and it is likely that these will form a list of "potentials" used by the instructor.   Then, too, there are certain classic topics which appear year after year in various disguises, such as questions concerning third party beneficiaries or assignment in contracts; manufacturer's liability or contributory negligence in tort. Such will rank high on the list of potentials.   Then, too, some help may be gained from scanning previous examinations set in the course by the particular instructor.   Barring the possibility that he will use the same question two years in succession, the perusal of the old examinations may give you some clues as to what to expect.   Finally, it is wise to run through the recent decisions on the subject in your jurisdiction or in the federal courts, because sometimes these decisions form the basis for questions either in law school or on bar examinations.

We have already said that in effect you actually begin to prepare for the examination on the first day of the course. This means constant and faithful preparation of abstracts or briefs, attention to discussion in class, regular review, and integration. There will be times when you do not understand the cases studied or when you cannot follow the trend of the class discussion. Note these points down and as soon as possible, while the matter is still fresh in your mind, attempt to clarify it by additional reading or by questions. Do not put the matter off, because you will find that the instructor is more open to questioning on current assignments than on one which you have had six weeks ago.

The examination period. You should remember that during the examination period it is usual for you to be examined on several subjects in the space of a few days. This means that it is necessary for you to allow sufficient time to review all of these courses and not merely to concentrate on one alone. You will find that some courses and some instructors are more demanding than others, and so you will be tempted to put all of your time into these courses, but you must recall that the other courses must be passed successfully as well. You may also discover to your sorrow that some instructors who seemingly were not demanding in class become exceedingly demanding at the time of examinations. The only way to learn these things except by painful experience is to consult with the upperclassmen about the folklore of the various instructors.

There are many theories about the night before examinations. There is no binding rule. Some maintain that the best way is to close the books, go to a movie, and turn in early.   Others maintain that the last night is the best night for cramming.   Both theories have produced passes and failures.   For the man who has done his review faithfully and well, it is possible to go to a movie with a clear conscience and achieve relaxation.   For the man who is not prepared, the last night's cram may do the trick or it may render him drugged and dull in the morning.   Whatever theory you pursue, the essential thing is that you go to the examination with a clear head, a flexible mind, plenty of ink in your pen, and some scratch paper.

In examinations, as in many other things, the approach to the business is important.   There are men who frankly "blow up" or "draw a blank" because they have become so tense at the prospect of examinations that their whole thought-process is fear-blocked and they make unnecessary errors. The man who can develop a pill for this complex will have made for himself a fortune, but to date there is no such pill and the cure must be effected by the examinee himself.

Since the examination is normally limited as to time allowed, and since usually the time is insufficient to permit extended development of all the questions, the element of pressure is present.   Some people react quite calmly to pressure, while others tend to go into panic.   There are many mottoes which could be quoted, but the real difficulty with the advice "Keep cool" is putting it into practice.   However, since one cannot do all the answers exhaustively, it becomes necessary to choose those issues which are most important and to concentrate on them, leaving the minor issues to more cursory treatment.   Actually, one of the reasons given for the limitation of time in examinations is that it forces the student to make a selection among major and minor points involved.

Read the instructions carefully. It is a sad but true fact that despite all our educational improvements many students seem incapable of reading correctly. It is probable that the instructor spent considerable time in wording the questions so as to avoid ambiguity. Therefore, the instructions should be read with equal care. Does he warn you that all questions must be attempted in the time allotted? Note particularly that part of the question which states what you are required to do. If the question states, "Advise the defendant as to his rights," then that is your task. No matter how clever an answer you may make as to the rights of someone else, it will avail you nothing if that is not what was asked. Sometimes the question may state, "Discuss the possible legal actions involved in these facts." This allows you greater latitude, but it is still a specific question. It cannot be said too often, even though year after year it falls on some deaf ears, that the answer must be responsive to the question asked. It is part of a lawyer's training to be able to answer directly to direct questions. Anyone who has marked examination papers can give you examples of the men who write voluminously, opening up the flood gates of pent-up knowledge, but who unfortunately fail to hit the matter involved.

Think before you write. There are students who, having glanced cursorily at the question, begin to write immediately whatever comes into their heads, with no reflection and little thought of organization. There is an unpleasant name sometimes given to such answers. Sometimes, these students discover midway through the answer that they have misread the question and much valuable time has been lost. It is important to remember that in answering the question, your primary task is to write so as to convince the instructor that you have understood the legal issues concerned, that you know the legal tools by which they can be approached and solved, and that you show sufficient ability at all this to be turned loose upon the public as a practitioner. If this aim is kept in mind, it becomes apparent that a well reasoned, carefully thought out and expressed answer is more apt to carry conviction than one which rambles all around Robin Hood's barn before approaching the problem at all. Consequently, you should think through the whole question, outline your tactics, plan your attack, and then begin to write.

But even here another word of warning must be given. However logical and sound your thinking about the problem may be, and however acceptable your tactics may be in your scratch outline, unless that thought-process, that organization, that logic gets put down into understandable word symbols on the examination paper, you may not get credit for it. An unexpressed thought does not carry conviction outside the holder thereof. Hence, perhaps our caption should be rephrased to read: *think before you write and write what you think.*

It is true that the student possessing a minimum of information and a facile style of writing plus an ability to use that minimum effectively may do better on an examination than one who possesses far more information but who, when faced by the necessity of putting it in writing, does a miserable job. The psychologist may someday answer this problem. Meanwhile, as the system now stands, it is necessary for a man to be fluent in writing skill if he is to do well in law school examinations. These are necessary hurdles; the man who wants to jump them, but who has not yet developed the skill, must practice.

Something should now be said about *the approach to the examination question itself.* Usually it is phrased as a given fact-situation involving named parties.   These facts must be read with great care.   In some instances, it may help to set them out on scratch paper in chronological order so that you can see the sequence of events.   Remember that you must work within the ambit of these given facts.   To assume more facts is to change the picture and so perhaps reach a wrong diagnosis.   The instructor has considered that these facts are sufficient to enable you to work.   Only in the event that the instructor gives you permission to do so, should they be altered in any way.

Now, having read these facts carefully, you will select from the stated facts those which have legal significance. For example, suppose that the facts state that A, aged 27, wearing a Brooks Brothers suit, was driving a motorcar at the rate of 85 miles per hour.   The facts of his age, speed, and means of conveyance may be of importance; what he was wearing is surplus detail.   Frequently, this selection can be made by underscoring on your paper the facts which have legal significance, so that the underscored portions will form a pattern as you look at the question.

From a study of these important facts, you should discover the legal points or issues raised in the question.   Some of these you will treat as major points and some as minor.   Now, having discovered the legal issues which are raised, turn to find out exactly what the instructor asks about these legal problems.   By this means you will understand both what the problem is and what you are expected to do about it.

The next step is to marshal for your use the law rules you have learned and to select as tools those which are applicable to the problems at hand.   By applying these tools you can reach certain hypotheses with regard to the question asked. For example, you may come to the informed guess that A has a possible action against B for damages for false im-

prisonment. This may well be the first bit of writing you
have actually done on the examination paper, although into
the making of this statement has gone much preliminary
thought.

This being your hypothesis, you should then turn to the
writing out of the proof. If the action be for false imprisonment, then in order to prevail you must demonstrate
from the stated facts that the elements of false imprisonment
as a cause of action (learned from the law rules) are present.
You must further demonstrate that none of the available
defenses (learned also from the law rules) are available from
the facts. Where the law rules as learned are ambiguous or
in conflict, then you must state the various positions and attempt a resolution of them. This course of analysis and
synthesis must be written down. It forms the "meat" of the
answer. It is evidence that you are able to use the legal
method and to integrate usefully the given facts with the
propositions of law already laid down.

Then, having made your hypothesis and having checked
it by all the learned law rules and approaches, you are ready
to reach a conclusion on the matter. For example, you
may conclude that A's action against B for damages for
false imprisonment will prevail. Whether or not the conclusion will be deemed correct depends upon the instructor.
Some instructors set their questions on the assumption that
there is a right and a wrong answer. In such a case, your
conclusion must coincide with that reached by the instructor
in his analysis. Other instructors set questions on the assumption that there is no inevitably right answer and so invite a full discussion as a means of enabling them to determine
the size and scope of your grasp of a legal problem. It is
part of your training as a law student to "size up" the in-

structor and his method, just as later you will "size up" a judge or jury or opposing counsel.

It is always wise to *read over your answer*. Remember that it is what you have written and not what you intended to write which the instructor judges. However careful you may be, it is always possible that under stress or in haste you have omitted written discussion of a point which you thought about, or you may have transposed words so that they say the opposite of what you meant, or you may have failed to set out ideas which you had jotted down on your scratch notes for discussion. A few minutes' proofreading may mean the difference between a passing and a failing paper.

Once the examination is over, forget it. By this is meant that "post mortems" never can help the examination and they seldom do anything for the student except to make him annoyed with himself. There are more examinations to be taken, and it is well to concentrate on them and let the "dead past bury its dead." The only kind of post mortem which is useful is that which is done with the instructor. He may point out to you the defects which can be cured, so that you can learn from your mistakes.

THE LAWYER AND HIS ETHICS

In this book we have had much to say of tools and techniques and method, the "how" of becoming a trained lawyer. This is important. However, it is only a part of legal education. For <u>education is more than mere training in skills and techniques</u>. If it were that alone, we might enroll precocious chimpanzees in our courses. Legal education, to be worthy of that name, must be concerned with the way in which and the ends for which the tools are to be used. By this is not meant simply that courses in legal ethics should be given; rather we mean that the concept of purpose should be a part of each course, of each problem.

Each of us at some time must answer the question, What am I building with the tools which have been given to me? Am I simply preparing a brief? Am I representing a client? Am I seeking to protect man's rights and to see that justice is done?

Law study is the period of acquiring the tools of the profession, the ideas, the values, the rules, the skills, and the techniques. Law schools and bar examiners will test us to see that we possess these tools in sufficient quantity and that we understand the nature of their use. <u>But tools in themselves are neutra</u>l. They are for use. And it is man who supplies the purpose, who decides what is to be built. We have been given the tools. Now it is up to us to build.

Any book concerning the practice of law and ethics must

meet two questions or challenges if it is to carry conviction. The questions are much the same as were asked of Socrates and yet they are also as new as today's newspaper. What assurance is there that the following of ethical standards will bring any reward? Are not ethics an expensive luxury to be indulged in only by men with fat retainers in their pockets or by philosophers far removed from the market place?

It has been said that ethics is something which should be taught to the young men and returned to and mulled over by the old. What then of the middle years when man is most active? It is perhaps true that there are some lawyers who have achieved both financial success and acclaim although some of their actions would not pass the test of ethical standards. It may be true that there are lawyers in practice who by all accounts should have been disbarred but have not been. It is certainly true that in the field of law, as in other areas of activity, the *mêlée* of competition has rendered it difficult to avoid the compromising of standards. Some young lawyers tell their law teachers that they were taught how law ought to be practiced but not how it is actually practiced, thus laying grounds for cynicism and disillusionment. Little is to be gained by blinding ourselves to these challenges. To the extent that they are true, they constitute a stain upon the legal profession. But by the same token, little is to be gained by assuming that these challenges represent the whole picture.

Let us try, then, to look at the whole picture. The profession of law is composed of all those men and women who in their own right are qualified as members of the Bar. Each of these is held to know and has sworn to abide by the canons of ethics of the profession. In their most widely accepted form in this country, these are found in the Canons of Professional Ethics of the American Bar Association.

Each of these persons has an understanding in his own conscience of that which he believes to be his obligation, as a lawyer, to his clients, to the courts, to his fellow lawyers, to law and justice. The great majority of these people conduct their work as lawyers in accordance with the prescribed ethics of their profession. A minority do not. Some of those who do not are disbarred or otherwise disciplined by the profession. Some manage in one way or another to escape detection or punishment. But even those who escape actual discipline frequently suffer the disapproval of their fellow lawyers, of judges, or of the society in which they live. Aroused and vigilant public opinion is still a powerful regulator of man's acts. The important thing in the whole picture is not that there are malefactors and that some of them escape punishment, though this is to be regretted. The important thing is that malefactors are the exception and not the rule; that the profession of law as a whole is ashamed of these lapses and realizes that its position of honor suffers by reason of them.

What, then, shall we say of the ethics of our profession? The position is sometimes taken that it is unnecessary to write about ethics for the lawyer because they are or ought to be the same as for any other right-thinking member of the community. To an extent this is true, and yet the lawyer is not just an ordinary member of the community. He is a *dedicated* man, and it is this dedication which sets him off and lays upon him the special call to high standards.

The essence of the lawyer's position is that he acts under a trust—a trust laid upon him by the community and state in admitting him to the profession, by the courts in which he is privileged to appear and plead causes, by the clients whose affairs he manages and whose interests he protects, and by the ideals which he has voluntarily sworn to uphold, foster, and cherish. In the Preamble to the American Bar Association's Canons of Professional Ethics we are reminded that "the future of the Republic, to a great extent, depends upon our maintenance of Justice pure and unsullied" and that this "cannot be maintained unless the conduct and the motives of the members of our profession are such as to merit the approval of all just men." Lawyers are not the only people who act under trust. Clergymen, doctors, and public officials also act under trust. They too are dedicated men.

It is easy to say that a man acts under a trust, but one must also inquire as to the obligations which are implied by the trust. Sometimes it is said that the integrity of a nation can be determined by the character of the obligations implied in the terms "trust" and "good faith." There is an old story of the king who had three sons, to each of whom he gave a certain sum of money which was to be held in trust and for which each was to render an accounting. The first son took the money and buried it in the earth in a safe place, and at the end of the period set by the king he dug up the money and returned it. The second son took the money and mingled it with his own funds, giving it no more or less care than he gave to his own possessions, and at the end of the period he too returned to the king the exact sum of money. The third son set the money aside and invested it with care greater even than that which he bestowed upon his own fortune so that at the end of the period he returned to his father, the king, not only the sum with which he had been entrusted, but an increase as well. And we are told that the king returned to the third son both his original portion and those of his brothers. Each man had acted under the same instructions. Each man had kept the fund safe. But the third son alone had seen in the fact of trust an added obligation.

The lawyer, like the third son, is to act with respect to

matters undertaken, not simply with that degree of care which he normally bestows upon his own affairs, but with a special care which arises from both the terms of the trust and the standards of his profession. This does not mean that we exact from a lawyer a superhuman skill or that we measure him against a paragon of virtues. We expect him to bring to his task care commensurate with the circumstances involved and the standards of morally responsible members of the professional community.

This means, for example, that lawyers administering funds entrusted to them must use greater care than that which they would use with their own funds. These funds do not belong to the lawyer. If known risks are involved, they should be taken only after consultation with the client in which the client has the aid of his counsel's advice. This means, for example, that matters disclosed to the lawyer in a lawyer-client relationship are matters received and held in confidence and are not to be revealed without permission of the client. It is true that if in the course of this relationship the client relates to the lawyer information which convinces the lawyer of the illegality or impropriety of his client's case, the lawyer may withdraw. However, it does not follow that the attorney is then free to divulge such information, except that by Canon 37 "the announced intention of a client to commit a crime is not included within the confidences which he (the lawyer) is bound to respect."

This obligation also implies that the sound lawyer will not discuss his client's case with those who are not directly concerned with it, nor will he discuss any of the affairs of his client with outsiders. Such information is normally protected within the lawyer-client privilege. It is true that such obligations as we have just discussed are not peculiar to lawyers. The doctor and priest or minister likewise accept such obligations by virtue of their dedicated service. There are sound reasons for this obligation. The lawyer or doctor who abuses the confidence reposed in him is not likely to be trusted again. Communities are not slow to learn which of their members are capable of trust and which gossip about the private affairs of others. Lawyers, like doctors, trade not only upon their reputation for technical skill but also upon their reputation for honesty, integrity, and performance under trust.

The notion of trust and dedication also implies obligations to the courts and other agencies charged with the administration of law and settlement of disputes. These agencies are entitled to courtesy, respect, candor, and fairness. It may be that the judge as a man does not merit respect, but the court as an institution in our society is to be respected. This does not mean that lawyers are forbidden to take action against judicial officers who act improperly, because Canon 1 advises us that "whenever there is proper ground for serious complaint of a judicial officer, it is the right and duty of the lawyer to submit his grievance to the proper authorities." This requirement of respect for the institution is not a phenomenon peculiar to legal circles. The salute given to an officer of superior rank is not given to the man as such but to the institution which his uniform and rank represent. The respect which is to be shown to the President of the United States is rendered to the office regardless of one's personal views as to the individual merits of the occupant of the office. There are those who challenge the rightness of these propositions, but under our system of thought such customs are imperative if the institutions are to be preserved. For this reason, among others, courts are given the power to punish those who fail to observe these obligations to the court.

The requirement of candor and fairness is difficult to define precisely. The court is entitled to the advice of counsel as to the law involved in a case, in the form of either briefs or oral argument. The court is entitled to the orderly presentation of evidence before the court and to the observance by the counsel of legal restrictions and amenities in dealing with the court, witnesses, and opposing counsel. Intentional suppression by counsel of fact or law, or intentional falsification by counsel of fact or law, clearly violates the requirement of candor and fairness. The difficulty lies in knowing when such action is intentional and when it arises from honest doubt or ignorance.

It is well known that lawyers are not all equal in skill or intelligence. Clients distinguish among lawyers on this basis and sometimes expect the superior skill or knowledge of counsel to make up for certain organic weaknesses in their contentions. Or again, the funds at the disposal of one client sometimes make it possible for his lawyer to use methods of investigation and inquiry which the opposing lawyer may not be able to pursue. What, then, can we say of the duty of the lawyer whose case is strengthened by the ineptness or incompleteness of research of opposing counsel? Is one lawyer under an obligation to rectify for the court mistakes made by opposing counsel where to do so endangers his own client's case? These are not easy questions. Pious statements of ideal action are not enough unless they take into account the practical difficulties present in translating the ideals into specific problems and answers. A simple statement that the mores of the community decide such matters is not enough if the lawyer is to continue to merit a special position of trust in the community. Reference to individual conscience, trite though it may sound, is the only truthful answer. As Canon 18 reminds us, "the client cannot be made the keeper of the lawyer's conscience in professional matters."

We have spoken of the obligations to his client and to the courts as involved in the lawyer's trust. There is also the obligation of fair play to his fellow lawyers. It is sometimes said, unfortunately with more than a modicum of justification, that associations of lawyers have devoted the greater portion of their attention to the policing of these duties. The cries of "ambulance chaser" and "shyster" often rally more enthusiastic response for reform than proposals for "raising the ethical standards of the Bar" or investigating alleged "breaches of trust." That this is so stems at least in part from a failure to distinguish between legal ethics as moral standards and legal ethics as established professional practices. Much of that which passes as a discussion of legal ethics is in fact a discussion of professional custom and practice. The two may be related, but they also may constitute quite different problems. For example, the professional customs of limited advertising by lawyers or of the observance of minimum fee schedules are professional practices which concern lawyers as lawyers, but do not necessarily involve ethics in the sense of moral standards or principle. To include too much under the umbrella of "legal ethics" may ultimately be to discredit the concept itself and to invite the charge that lawyers are unethical persons. Lawyers should not need to be reminded that passing a law about a subject does not necessarily assure a change in reluctant mores. Thus, there is no intention in this chapter to discuss professional customs. We would simply point out that the obligation of fair play to one's fellow lawyers covers the honoring of promises given, common courtesy, and an awareness that truth and good faith are not the indisputable possessions of one man alone.

Throughout this discussion, it must be apparent that we have been presenting a single problem as seen on various levels: the legal ethics prescribed and ordered by the profession to which the lawyer has dedicated himself; the customs and practices pursued in concert by the members of the profession; and the ethical problems which arise because of the way in which the individual lawyer views the profession he has sworn to serve. It is this latter aspect which we must now discuss. To many it is the most important of the three and gives meaning to the others.

The ethics which a man uses in his profession are not apt to be vastly different from those by which he regulates his own life as a whole. For the man who possesses a high sense of personal honor and integrity, the prescribed ethical standards of his profession will occasion little difficulty, since compliance with the one arises from much the same cause as the other. For the man whose personal ethics are below those prescribed for his profession, the problem of compliance will present conflict. Let us take certain examples. There is the ageless question of the obligation of the lawyer to a client in whose case the lawyer does not believe. We have pointed out earlier that if the lawyer discovers that his client has in fact committed the illegal act with which he is charged or that the course of action which his client pursues is an illegal one, the lawyer has the right to refuse the case or to withdraw at any time from the case. There is no professional obligation upon the lawyer to continue in the attorney-client relationship in such a case. However, Canon 5 of the Canons of Professional Ethics of the American Bar Association points out that "it is the right of the lawyer to undertake the defense of a person accused of crime, regardless of his personal opinion as to the guilt of the accused; otherwise innocent persons, victims only of suspicious circumstances, might be denied proper defense." The Canon continues that "having undertaken such defense, the lawyer is bound, by all fair and honorable means, to present every defense that the law of the land permits, to the end that no person may be deprived of life or liberty, but by due process of law." Here, then, is the solution on the level of professional ethics. Whether this position is acceptable on the level of personal ethics depends upon the individual conscience.

Turning to a less dramatic but nonetheless important aspect of the same question, what of the case where the course of action proposed by the client offends the opinions and views of the lawyer as to what the law should be but does not necessarily conflict with what the law is? Should the lawyer who is convinced of the validity and soundness of a legislative enactment undertake at the request of a client a suit which may result in having the law declared invalid because of a technical irregularity? Should the lawyer who firmly believes in the rights of labor undertake a case for an employer anxious to defeat or circumvent those rights? These are questions which have perplexed young, middle-aged, and old lawyers at some time or other. Canon 31 is quite clear that "no lawyer is obliged to act either as adviser or advocate for every person who may wish to become his client. He has the right to decline employment. Every lawyer upon his own responsibility must decide what employment he will accept as counsel, what causes he will bring into court for plaintiffs, what cases he will contest in court for defendants." Canon 15 reminds us that the lawyer is to "obey his own conscience and not that of his client."

Your answer to these problems will depend to a considerable degree on your approach to another question, namely, What does my profession mean to me? Is it a job indistinguishable from any other job except in the specific tasks involved? If so, one client may appear much like another, except that some may be less demanding of your time than others and some may pay your fees more promptly than others. Under such a thought-process, you, like many another employee, do the task in front of you and let someone else worry whether or not it is just, socially desirable, and economically sound. But if that be all that your profession means to you, then perhaps you might better be a plumber or bricklayer—in which ethical value-judgments may play second fiddle to technical competence. Is your profession merely a means for making a livelihood? To make a living is both necessary and important to most of us, but this should not be the primary aim of the profession of law as a dedicated service. Is your profession chosen simply because it has about it the aura of respectability? If so, then one must recall that such reputations require constant nurture. Or is your work seen as a high calling to minister to the needs of your fellow man? Is it seen as some sort of crusade?

Your answers to such questions as these may in turn depend upon your answer to another question: What do I want my life to be? What are the values which have lasting meaning for me? The point of all this is that many of the problems which we treat loosely under the title "legal ethics" are really problems of personal ethics manifesting themselves in the day-by-day practice of law. Those of us who see in law a high calling, a dedicated service, may see in a problem conflicts of ethical values which for another do not appear. This has always been so. Such does not make the problems easier. It merely calls attention to their true nature.

The profession of law has a great and honored name. This reputation has been earned because in the critical periods of history the members of this profession have stood for the protection of individual liberties and for the preservation of the ideals of truth, honor, justice, and integrity. Despite the fact that the profession has numbered among its members some scoundrels and perverters of justice, these have been the exceptions and not the rule.

But no reputation endures forever without attention to the sources from which it springs. Reputations are ephemeral. If they are to be kept healthy and sound, they must be watered by good deeds and constant devotion. It is far easier to destroy a good reputation than to build one. The devotion of a profession to ideals less than the highest will ultimately bring a reputation less than the highest. It is the special charge laid upon each generation of lawyers to see that the ideals for which they stand are those which in the long sweep of history will be pronounced sound.

Much of modern teaching, as indeed much of this book, is devoted to accenting the skills, methods, and techniques, the possession of which marks the capable lawyer. These are the means, the tools, but they must not be mistaken for the ends. As means, they can be used toward the accomplishment of evil as well as good. The nitrates which contribute to the enrichment of the soil can also cause the destruction of man. The lawyer is judged not only by his skill but also by the ends which he espouses. By oath sworn and tradition inherited, the lawyer assumes a major responsibility for the ends of the society in which he lives. These are commonly called justice, truth, honor, and integrity. For the stewardship of these ideals, the lawyer must answer to himself, his fellow man, and his Creator. To the extent to which you pursue these ends, you will help the profession of law to remain an honored one and you will fulfil your oath and your chosen mission.

INDEX